British Aircraft Carriers

by

W. D. G. Blundell

Published by

Model & Allied Publications Ltd.

13-35 Bridge Street, Hemel Hempstead, Herts.

1969

By the same author:

    Ships of the Modern Royal Navy

    Jane's Fighting Ships 1968-9 (all countries except Europe and the U.S.A.)

Other titles from the M.A.P. range include:

    Model Racing Yachts

    Power Model Boats

    Boat Modelling

    The Anatomy of Nelson's Ships

    Modelling the Revenge

    Seventeenth Century Rigging

    Flags for Ship Modellers

    Period Ship Modelling

    Secrets of Ships in Bottles

A complete list of all titles is available from the publishers

Trade Distributors:

ARGUS PRESS LTD.

12-18 Paul Street, London, E.C.2

Printed in Great Britain by
Percy Brothers Limited, The Hotspur Press, Manchester, M60 IPB and
145 Fleet Street, London, E.C.4

A*

Contents

The author wishes to acknowledge and thank the Ministry of Defence (Navy) for supplying notes, drawings and photographs and giving permission to reproduce many excellent photographs, and the Imperial War Museum photographic staff for supplying some rare and historic photographs.

The first-ever carrier landing

4

Introduction

ALTHOUGH many volumes have been written about British Naval Aviation, to the best of my knowledge, there has never been one dealing specifically with the ships that made the record possible. In this book will be found histories, photographs and—that which is rarely seen— scale drawings of every ship that played a major part. The men must always come before the ships but their glorious deeds have been, very rightly, recognised and recorded elsewhere. Collectively the ships have been neglected and I hope, in some small measure, to correct this omission.

Many years ago the initial idea of this book came to me during a blustery August afternoon in the English Channel on board H.M.S. Theseus. Our Firefly and Sea Fury aircraft had just landed on before we set heading for the Far East and the Korean War. As a very junior aircraft maintenance rating I was detailed to sit in a cockpit to operate the brakes.

Uncomfortably near the edge of the rear flight deck I felt somewhat apprehensive as the ship corkscrewed (in my position this motion was greatly magnified) westwards. Just as I was beginning to feel convinced that an early watery grave was my destiny, commonsense took control. My position was not unique at all and there was no real need for me to feel concerned—for many years the Royal Navy had been operating carriers in far worse conditions and knew what it was about. Relaxed by this knowledge, my mind turned to those earlier carriers that, almost certainly, had passed this way. Intrigued with this idea, I thought, one day in the distant future, I would like to compile a book about them.

Here, at last, is that long overdue book. Perhaps it is more appropriate coming at this time for, unless future defence policy is radically changed, the aircraft carrier will pass out of the Royal Navy in less than ten years time. No more carriers are planned to be built in this country although, it is just possible, one or two may be acquired from the U.S. Navy to supplement our own ageing ships—there has not been a British carrier laid down for over twenty years! This book then, more than likely, covers the complete history of the British aircraft carriers.

W. D. G. BLUNDELL

The Aircraft Carrier 1911—1969

WHAT was the first aircraft carrier? This is a question that I have often been asked. It could be answered in the late Professor Joad manner by saying—it all depends on what is meant by an aircraft carrier. Do we mean a ship that carried aeroplanes with wheels for an under-carriage? Or can we count seaplanes with their floats? Obviously if the latter category is taken into account we can go back many more years. For the purpose of this book I will be considering both types—after all both fall within the generic term aircraft, the only real difference between them is their alighting gear. However, to answer the question adequately, I should like to quote the following from an official Admiralty document.

'H.M.S. *Argus* was the first ship of the Royal Navy to have been designed as an aircraft carrier, earlier ships having been improvised from other types. Previously there had been the *Hermes*, a light cruiser, which in 1913 was adapted as a seaplane carrier; the *Ark Royal*, a merchant ship purchased while building in 1914; cross-Channel steamers such as the *Engadine*, which sent up a seaplane at the Battle of Jutland; and other adaptations such as the Cunard Liner *Campania*, which served with the Grand Fleet until lost after collision in a gale in 1918'.

The *Argus* was in fact laid down as an Italian liner originally but converted to an aircraft carrier during construction. More information about this ship will be found on later pages.

In the beginning, the British concentrated their efforts on the seaplane—also included in this term is the more landbased flying boat—and ships that could be adapted to carry them. Nobody denied the advantages of aircraft that would extend the seeing eye of the fleet although, it must be admitted, there were many who thought the frail, clumsy craft were more nuisance than their practical worth. To land and take off these aircraft had to use the sea, and unless it was comparatively calm this was not a practical proposition. In any event the parent ship would have to stop when recovering or lowering her aircraft; she would certainly be a sitting duck for the submarine which was beginning to grow out of its infancy. Generally speaking, the service began to think that, as the seaplane could only operate from calmish, sheltered seas, the seaplane carrier would be more of a land-bound depot ship than an active part of the fleet.

Of course, if an aircraft could take off from a ship and, better still, land on her while under way, then that would be a different story. It took an American, Eugene Ely, to point the way. On the 14th November, 1910, he flew a Curtiss biplane off the U.S.S. *Birmingham*, to enable him to do which a platform of 57 ft. had been erected on the forecastle. A few weeks later, the 18th January, 1911, he succeeded in landing on board the U.S.S. *Pennsylvania*; this time a longer platform, 120 ft., had been erected at the stern of the ship. It is also interesting to note that arrestor wires—sand bags were at each end of the wires—were used, and also a canvas screen at the end of the landing run was available as a crash barrier.

These experiments were followed by the British with intense interest and a year later the first aircraft take-off from a British warship was made. The ship was an old battleship, H.M.S. *Hibernia*, at anchor; a few months later, May 1912, the first take-off from a ship under way was made—H.M.S. *Africa*, a sister ship of the *Hibernia*. In 1913 H.M.S. *Hermes*, an old cruiser not to be confused with subsequent carriers of this name, was also given a forward flying plat-form and carried two seaplanes with wheels for taking off as well as floats. However, these ships had had this equipment removed by the outbreak of war. Future development of the air-craft carrier was governed by the evolution of the aircraft and the availability of suitable ships for conversion.

The first ship ever to be completed as a pure seaplane carrier was H.M.S. *Ark Royal*, which had been laid down as a collier and was converted while building. Cranes lifted the seaplanes, carried in the holds, into the water for take-off and recovered them again after landing. Then came, between 1914 and 1917, the much faster cross - channel steamers *Empress, Engadine, Riviera, Ben-My-Chree, Manxman, Vindex, Pegasus, Nairana* and the much larger Cunard liner, *Campania*. The first successful take-off by an aircraft with wheeled floats was made from the *Campania* in August 1915. About this time an aircraft from the *Ben-My-Chree* made history by carrying out the first effective aerial torpedo attack in the Dardanelles. Three months later a land aeroplane took off from the *Vindex* and gradually the seaplane, with its cumbersome floats, was replaced by the aeroplane.

Gradually, as the war progressed, the role of aircraft increased in importance; at the commencement of hostilities it was generally thought that aircraft would only be suitable for reconnaissance and spotting for artillery. Perhaps this was understandable with the early, flimsy built aircraft which just could not carry much in the way of offensive weapons and equipment; however, the aircraft was growing up, it was becoming sturdier, faster, larger and most important of all it was becoming more reliable. It was also becoming increasingly obvious that our early attempts at making aircraft carriers—in reality seaplane carriers with a flying platform forward for take-offs—were just not adequate; to rectify this situation warships were converted to aircraft carriers and a lot of thought, based on experience and experiment, went into their design.

In March 1918 the *Furious*, formerly a large light cruiser armed with 18-in. guns, emerged fully converted as a carrier. Seven aircraft from this ship carried out a successful raid on Tondern Zeppelin base, July 1918, and destroyed two enemy airships. On the 2nd August, 1918, the first successful aircraft landing was made on her foredeck by Squadron Commander E. H. Dunning, D.S.C., R.N.A.S.; unfortunately this officer was killed on his second landing as a tyre burst on touchdown and the aircraft went over the side. The way ahead had been shown and was clear now; the embryonic stage of the aircraft carrier was over. In October 1918 the *Vindictive*, laid down as the cruiser *Cavendish*, and the *Argus*, laid down as a liner, joined the fleet; before their usefulness could be proved the war was over.

At the end of the war two other carriers were under construction, the *Eagle* and the *Hermes*. Both were interesting ships and gave yeoman service to Naval Aviation until sunk in the Second World War. The *Eagle* was laid down as a battleship and, for construction purposes, it seemed impossible to the designers to do away with all the existing superstructure. Originally the intention had been to produce a completely flush decked ship along the lines of the *Argus*. It was suggested, by the designers, that the bridge superstructure should in principle remain but could be set on one side, thus leaving a clear run for the aircraft. Before the Admiralty committed themselves to this a dummy and experimental superstructure was rigged on the deck of the *Argus*; flight tests were made and, according to pilots' reports, the erection on the deck did not materially interfere with landings and take-offs. Eventually the *Eagle* appeared with what was called the 'island-type' superstructure, set on the starboard side, and a similar arrangement was made for the *Hermes*. Ever since the island-type carrier has been used.

Pride of place must go to the *Hermes* as the first ship designed from the keel up as an aircraft carrier. She was quite a small carrier, about 12,000 tons, with a shallow draught, and in consequence spent a lot of time in the Far East operating from the shallow harbours of China and the Pacific islands.

Following the successful experimental flying on board the *Furious* it was decided to convert two more similar ships—the *Courageous* and *Glorious*. These two ships were about the same size as the *Furious*, 22,000 tons, and carried four 15-in. guns as a main armament; they had been specially designed for operations in the shallow waters of the Frisian islands where other battleships and battle cruisers could not go because of their deeper draughts. In the event these operations never took place and these ships were something like 'white elephants' in the fleet after the war. When conversion to aircraft carriers was completed, in the early twenties, both ships looked very similar to the *Furious* except that they carried an island type superstructure incorporating the funnel and bridge on the starboard side.

Then followed the lean years of Naval Aviation. In many ways this was to be expected after 'a war to end all wars' had just been fought which had bled our economy nearly dry. With all three armed services trying to exist on the very limited amount of money available for defence purposes, with international disarmament talks and treaties taking place (Britain was

HMS Argus laid up in reserve in June 1947

fitted on to battleships and cruisers were given a thorough testing by this now obsolescent ship. In addition to catapult trials she also participated in experiments with the Heine mat—this was a German invention, the principle being that seaplanes taxied over a large slatted mat, which was then hauled up to the ship and the aircraft was hoisted on board; however, it was not a success and soon discarded. In 1934 it was decided to re-name the ship *Pegasus* and leave her proud original name open for a future aircraft carrier.

Compared with her First World War record the part played by the *Pegasus* in the Second World War was a lot less glamorous and significant. There was one active spell in early 1941 when she carried fighters that could be catapulted off to provide air cover for convoys. This only lasted for a very short time until the advent of the escort carrier. The rest of her service was spent as an accommodation ship until she was sold for merchant service in 1947. In 1950 she was scrapped after many years of long and useful service to naval aviation.

LEADING PARTICULARS
Displacement: 7,020 tons.
Dimensions: 366 ft. O.A., $50\frac{3}{4}$ ft. Beam, $17\frac{1}{2}$ ft. Mean Draught.
Engines: Triple Expansion, 3,000 H.P., 10·6 knots.
Armament: 10 Seaplanes, 4-12 pdr. Guns (originally), later mounted 20 mm.
Complement: 140 to 180.

(Imperial War Museum photo)

Empress

B*

Cross Channel Ships 1914-17

ALTHOUGH the *Ark Royal* was to prove an extremely useful ship throughout her long career, it was realised, almost from her inception, that she lacked one important characteristic—speed. It would be impossible for her, or similar ships, to keep up with the fleet at sea and operate as part of it. To overcome this shortcoming it was decided, shortly after the war began, to convert the very much faster— 20 knots plus, as opposed to 10 knots—cross-channel type of steamer.

The first three ships to be taken over were the *Engadine*, *Riviera* and *Empress*, which had been built for the South Eastern and Chatham Railway Company; in peacetime they had sailed from Dover and Folkestone to Boulogne and Calais. Their initial, hasty conversion was carried out at Chatham Dockyard to enable them to carry three Short seaplanes; there was no time to build a hangar and a canvas shelter had to suffice. Six months later, after practical experience in operating these ships had been gained, they were taken in hand by the Cunard Company for a more realistic conversion. A comparatively large hangar—it could hold four seaplanes with their wings folded—was erected aft of the two funnels; cranes—as opposed to cargo hoists—were fitted to facilitate the hoisting and lowering of the seaplanes, and armament, which included some of the first anti-aircraft guns, was mounted.

Three more, slightly larger, cross-channel steamers were acquired and converted on the lines of the earlier ships, they were: *Ben-My-Chree*, *Manxman* and *Vindex* (ex *Viking*). Later most of these ships were fitted with a flight deck, which extended from the bridge to the bows, for aircraft to take off from. At first these aircraft were seaplanes with a launching trolley, but later they were pure aeroplanes which had to make other arrangements to land! It is interesting to note that this principle was used again in the Second World War with the catapult equipped merchant ships.

Soon after the war had started the *Engadine*, *Riviera* and *Empress* took part in a raid on the German naval base at Cuxhaven. Unfortunately, this very first naval air attack was not effective in terms of damage to the enemy. Shortly after this action the *Engadine* was part of a force that tried to destroy the Zeppelin sheds at Tondern; once again the raid was not a success and, in fact, only one aircraft managed to reach the target area. Unreliability of the then frail aircraft and the inexperience of the aircrew, at this early stage of war and flying, were the biggest single factors for these failures. However, they pointed the way, years hence, to Taranto and Pearl Harbour.

At the commencement of the battle of Jutland, 31st May, 1916, the C.-in -C. of the British Fleet, Admiral Jellicoe, detailed the *Engadine* to launch a seaplane for a reconnaissance flight. Forty minutes later the seaplane reported, by wireless, the position and course of enemy cruisers and destroyers that were scouting ahead of their fleet; this was the first time in history that an enemy fleet had ever been sighted from the air. A broken fuel pipe, which occurred shortly after the sighting, forced the seaplane to return to her carrier. Bad weather prevented further flights for the rest of the battle; had this not been so, then the whole course of the battle might have been changed to a much greater advantage for the British.

Throughout the war aircraft from these ships did valuable, but little publicised, work on anti-submarine patrols; sitting in open cockpits over the North Sea and Western Atlantic on cold winter days was not a very pleasant task. In the warmer Mediterranean climate the *Ben-My-Chree* took part in the Dardanelles campaign; from her decks was launched the first effective aerial torpedo attack against a Turkish warship.

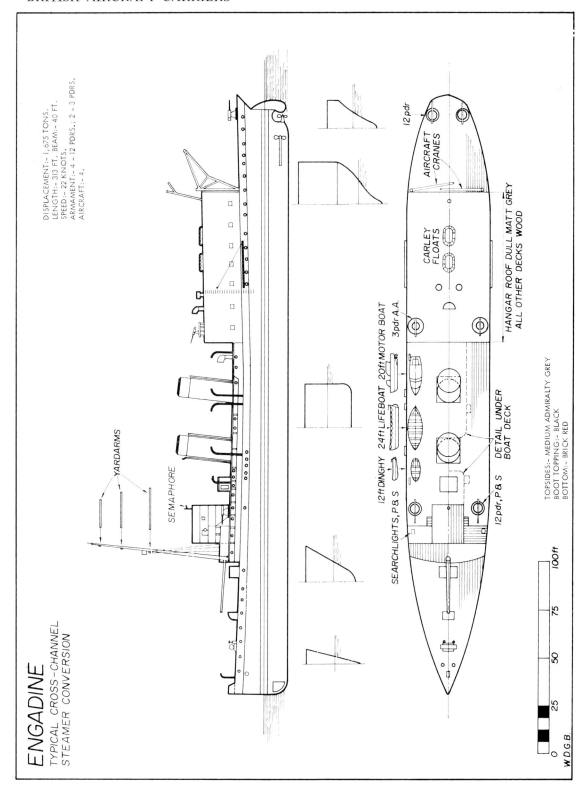

ENGADINE
TYPICAL CROSS-CHANNEL
STEAMER CONVERSION

DISPLACEMENT:- 1,675 TONS.
LENGTH:- 313 FT. BEAM:- 40 FT.
SPEED:- 22 KNOTS.
ARMAMENT:- 4 - 12 PDRS., 2 - 3 PDRS.
AIRCRAFT:- 4.

YARDARMS

SEMAPHORE

SEARCHLIGHTS, P & S

12ft DINGHY 24ft LIFEBOAT 20ft MOTOR BOAT

3 pdr. A.A.

12 pdr, P & S

DETAIL UNDER
BOAT DECK

12 pdr.

AIRCRAFT
CRANES

CARLEY
FLOATS

HANGAR ROOF DULL MATT GREY
ALL OTHER DECKS WOOD

TOPSIDES:- MEDIUM ADMIRALTY GREY
BOOT TOPPING:- BLACK
BOTTOM:- BRICK RED

W.D.G.B.

0   25   50   75   100 ft

(Imperial War Museum photo)

(Imperial War Museum photo)

Riviera

(Imperial War Museum photo)

Pegasus

Like the *Ark Royal*, she carried out spotting duties for the battleships' guns and reconnaissance flights. Until the advent of aircraft carriers with aeroplanes, much later in the war, most of the seaplane carriers served with the fleet at sea and enhanced its search capabilities considerably.

In addition to the cross-channel steamers, two other small passenger ships, the *Nairana* and *Pegasus*, were converted into aircraft carriers whilst building. These were similar ships to the cross-channel steamers but were intended to be used on the longer sea crossings to the continent; their length to beam ratio was less which gave them a somewhat dumpier appearance. Much of the experience gained with the earlier ships went into their conversion; the forward flight deck was a built-in feature and aeroplanes could be more adequately stowed and handled. Both ships saw service in the North Sea, White Sea and the Mediterranean.

When the war ended all the cross-channel steamers, with the exception of the *Ben-My-Chree*, were rapidly converted back to their peacetime role. The *Ben-My-Chree* and *Pegasus* were retained for a while as aircraft transports, the *Pegasus* until 1931, before being sold for passenger work.

LEADING PARTICULARS
Cross-Channel Steamers
Length: Varied between 311 and 375 ft. Beam: Varied between 40 and 46 ft.

Machinery: All turbines giving speeds between 21 and 24 knots.

Armament: Usually four 12pdr. plus six 3pdr. Anti-aircraft.

Aircraft: Four to six seaplanes and later included aeroplanes.

Complement: Around 250.

Displacement: *Ben-My-Chree* (2,651), *Empress* (1,694), *Engadine* (1,676) (gross tons), *Manxman* (2,174), *Riviera* (1,675), *Vindex* (1,951).

SHORT SEA SHIPS
Length: *Nairana*, 352 ft.; *Pegasus*, 332 ft.

Beam: *Nairana*, $45\frac{1}{2}$ ft.; *Pegasus*, 43 ft.

Machinery: Geared Turbines giving a speed of 20 to 21 knots.

Displacement: *Nairana*, 3,042 tons; *Pegasus*, 2,070 tons.

Armament: Two 12pdr.; two 12pdr. Anti-Aircraft.

Complement: Around 270.

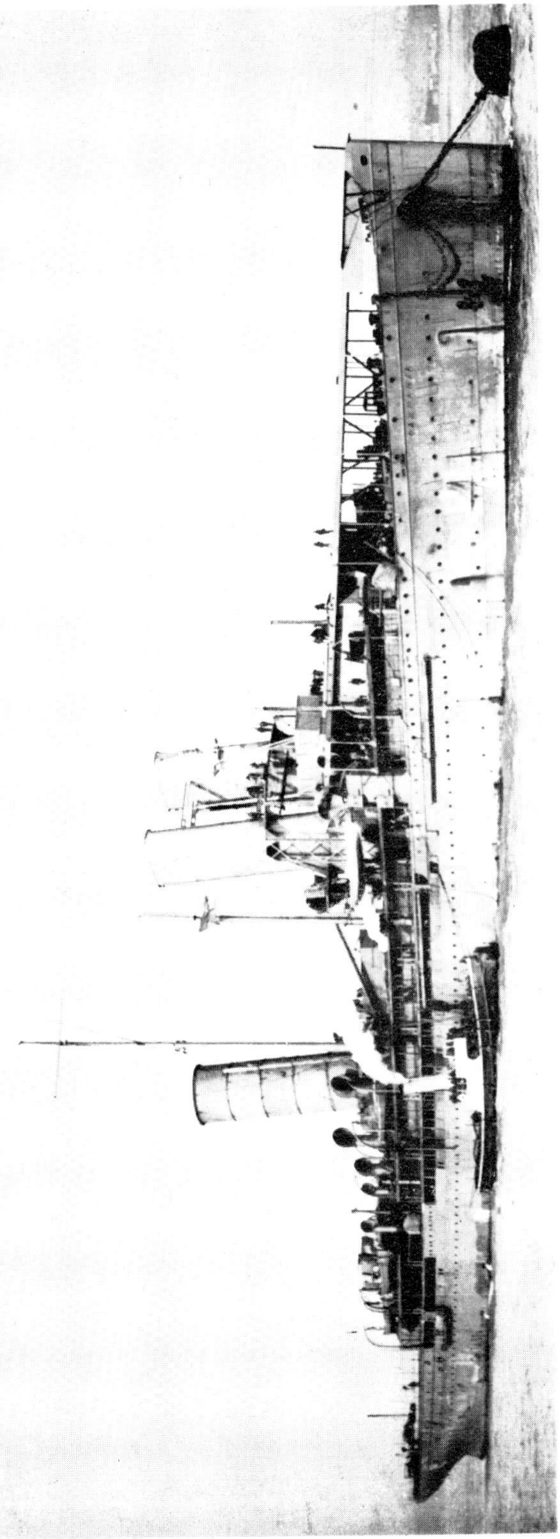

Campania

Campania

1915

A LONG time before the First World War, 1893 to be exact, the Cunard Company were very pleased to take delivery of their latest liner, the *Campania*. She set new standards of luxury travelling; more important perhaps, with her then very high speed of 22 knots she captured and held the coveted Blue Ribbon of the Atlantic for many years until the advent of larger and faster liners. At the outbreak of the war she was acquired by the Admiralty with the intention, like many other large and fast liners, of turning her into an armed merchant cruiser In the event, however, it was decided to convert her into a large seaplane carrier.

Large was, perhaps, a slight understatement! Twice the length and seven to eight times the displacement of the cross-channel steamers that had been converted, this ship represented a really serious effort to take naval aircraft to sea in force. Eleven seaplanes could be carried, as opposed to four in the earlier ships, and her cargo holds offered enough space to stow most of them below decks. With her high freeboard, a forward flying off deck was a practical proposition from the start; to make this deck even longer her front funnel was split into two separate ones mounted side by side. A substantial armament of six 4·7-in. guns was fitted.

Her first captain, when she was commissioned by the Royal Navy, was Commander Oliver Swann (later to be knighted and promoted to Air Marshal) who had been, in November 1911, the first British pilot ever to take a seaplane off the water. The first ever successful take-off by

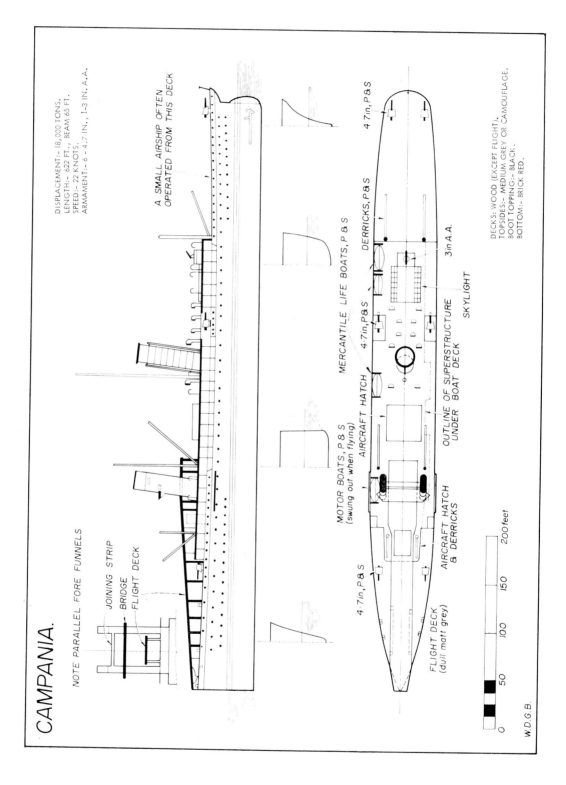

CAMPANIA.

NOTE PARALLEL FORE FUNNELS

JOINING STRIP
BRIDGE
FLIGHT DECK

DISPLACEMENT:- 18,000 TONS.
LENGTH:- 622 FT., BEAM 65 FT.
SPEED:- 22 KNOTS.
ARMAMENT:- 6 - 4.7 IN., 1-3 IN. A.A.

A SMALL AIRSHIP OFTEN
OPERATED FROM THIS DECK

MERCANTILE LIFE BOATS, P & S

4.7in, P&S

DERRICKS, P&S

3in A.A.

SKYLIGHT

AIRCRAFT HATCH

4.7in, P&S

OUTLINE OF SUPERSTRUCTURE
UNDER BOAT DECK

MOTOR BOATS, P & S
(swung out when flying)

AIRCRAFT HATCH
& DERRICKS

4.7in, P&S

FLIGHT DECK
(dull matt grey)

DECKS: WOOD (EXCEPT FLIGHT),
TOPSIDES:- MEDIUM GREY OR CAMOUFLAGE.
BOOT TOPPING:- BLACK.
BOTTOM:- BRICK RED.

0   50   100   150   200 feet

W.D.G.B.

24

(*Imperial War Museum photo*)

Campania in dazzle camouflage

(*Imperial War Museum photo*)

Campania in dazzle camouflage

(Imperial War Museum photo)

Skid landing on H.M.S. Furious

Furious   1917

NOT many people would have thought at the time of the *Furious*'s launch, 15th August, 1916, that her destiny lay with naval aviation. She had been laid down as a light battle cruiser specially designed for operations in shallower waters than normal ships of this type; to ensure her success in this she was to mount 18-in. guns. However, by the time she was being completed, there was no longer any requirement for the operations she had been designed for and the 18-in. gun was not a success. It was decided not to mount the forward 18-in. gun turret and she was completed with a flying off deck forward and a hangar under it. After a few months' service in this guise, June to November 1917, it was soon realised that

"FURIOUS". 10-7-42. 8 KTS.

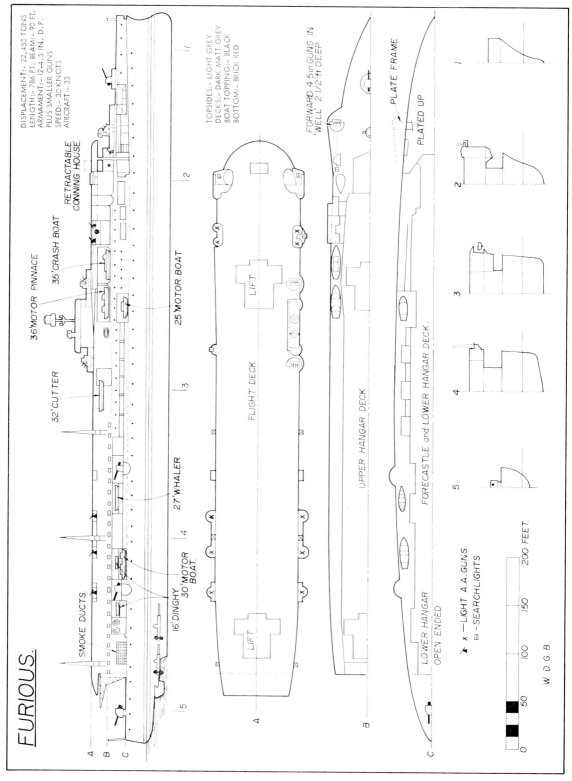

FURIOUS.

DISPLACEMENT:- 22,450 TONS
LENGTH:- 786 FT, BEAM:- 90 FT. D.P.
ARMAMENT:- 12-4.5 IN.
PLUS SMALLER GUNS
SPEED:- 30 KNOTS
AIRCRAFT:- 33

RETRACTABLE CONNING HOUSE.

36' MOTOR PINNACE

35' CRASH BOAT

25' MOTOR BOAT

32' CUTTER

27' WHALER

30' MOTOR BOAT.

16' DINGHY

SMOKE DUCTS.

TOPSIDES:- LIGHT GREY
DECKS:- DARK MATT GREY
BOAT TOPPING:- BLACK
BOTTOM:- BRICK RED

FORWARD 4.5in GUNS IN 'WELL' 2 1/2 ft DEEP

PLATE FRAME

PLATED UP

FLIGHT DECK

LIFT

UPPER HANGAR DECK

FORECASTLE and LOWER HANGAR DECK.

LOWER HANGAR
OPEN ENDED

x - LIGHT A.A. GUNS
☐ = SEARCHLIGHTS

0   50   100   150   200 FEET.

W.D.G.B

28

Furious in March 1942

considerable modifications were required to turn her into an efficient carrier.

Conversion was done rapidly—about three months—and included the removal of the after 18-in. gun turret; a landing deck with a hangar under it was built aft. On the 15th March, 1918, she was re-commissioned for the Grand Fleet as the flagship of Rear Admiral Sir Richard Phillimore, commanding the newly established 'Flying Squadron' until June 1919. She adequately proved her worth by giving the fleet extra eyes and air cover. One of her fighters shot down a German seaplane—19th June, 1918—and exactly one month later her aircraft bombed and destroyed the Zeppelin sheds at Tondern. (It will be recalled, from the article on cross-channel steamers, that much earlier on a similar raid had failed miserably). In their way these historic events were the forerunners, on a very small scale, of the great sea-air battles of World War Two.

Squadron Commander Dunning had shown the way, tragically, on to an aircraft carrier's flight deck but, with the bridge, mast and funnel remaining in the middle of the ship, it was still a hazardous business to land an aircraft on the short flight deck; if the aircraft did not stop in time it went into a barrier which resembled a giant football goal. Something had to be done about this landing-on problem; the only logical answer was a clear flight deck, free from any awkward protrusions. Between 1921 and 1925 this was done and, after extensive modification, the *Furious* appeared in her final guise, unrecognisable from the ship that had been laid down ten years before.

Along with the mere handful of other aircraft carriers that the Royal Navy possessed between the wars, she gave very useful service with the Home and Mediterranean Fleets. Many future captains of carriers spent part of their early careers in her; many of the lessons learnt from the peacetime carrier exercises were applied in the war to come. Just before the outbreak of the Second World War a mast and small superstructure were fitted on her starboard side; more modern anti-aircraft guns were mounted in this small refit.

When the war started the *Furious* was serving with the Home Fleet, based at Rosyth, and she was soon in action again. On the 22nd September, 1939, whilst on patrol, her aircraft attacked and probably seriously damaged an enemy submarine East of Fair Isle. Later in that year, with the battle cruiser *Repulse*, she formed the major part of a hunting group against U-boats in the Atlantic; 1939 finished with her forming

Furious, 1918

Furious in May, 1918

part of the escort of the large convoy, which brought to U.K. the first Canadian troops, that left Halifax on the 10th and arrived in the Clyde on the 17th December.

The next year of war began quietly enough, routine anti-submarine patrols and sweeps with the Home Fleet, but quickly warmed up with the Norwegian campaign. During April, May and June her aircraft, particularly her fighters, tried to give air cover—in the face of much greater numbers and more modern enemy aircraft—to the Allied force ashore. A near miss caused slight damage to her turbines, on the 18th April, during an enemy air attack off Tromso. However, she was able to repair this damage and was soon back in action for the rest of the campaign.

At the end of June 1940, she crossed the Atlantic to bring back aircraft from the U.S.A. to Britain, leaving Halifax on the 1st and arriving at Liverpool on the 7th July. In the September she took part in anti-shipping strikes at Tromso and Trondheim, Norway, and, during the latter attack, suffered some casualties and lost six aircraft; a similar operation was also carried out in October. On the 15th November, the *Furious* left Liverpool with R.A.F. aircraft for West Africa and was back at Liverpool on the 15th December. Later that month, while with a convoy bound for West Africa, she flew off aircraft in an attempt to locate the German cruiser *Admiral Hipper* which had attacked the convoy; however, this was unsuccessful owing to the low visibility that prevailed.

Nineteen forty-one began with more convoy work between Britain and West Africa; as well as providing air cover she also ferried many R.A.F. aircraft. At the time of the hunt for the *Bismarck* she was refitting at Belfast; while there, on the night of the 4th/5th May, a bomb dropped by an enemy aircraft passed through one of her hangars. It speaks much of the toughness of the ship and the wartime British shipbuilders when it is recorded that the *Furious* arrived, fully fit, at Gibraltar on the 12th May.

With the famous Force H and the *Ark Royal* she participated in an aircraft ferrying operation to Malta; she also took part in a similar operation in early July. At the end of July, and a long way from the sunny Mediterranean, she carried out an air attack on the port of Petsamo in Finland. Her aircraft found the harbour empty of shipping, but attacked the quays, oil tanks and the shipyard. Unfortunately, two Fulmars and one Albacore were lost as against one enemy aircraft. Early in August 1941 she took part in anti-shipping operations in Waranger

Fjord, Norway. On the 7th October she arrived at Philadelphia, U.S.A. for a much needed refit.

The *Furious* returned to Britain in April 1942, arriving in the Clyde on the 12th; she continued re-fitting and working up until July, when she rejoined the Home Fleet. Her first operations in 1942 were to ferry aircraft to Malta on the 11th and 17th August and, again, on the 29th October. In November, she took part in the North African landings—Operation 'Torch'. After this invasion she became part of Force H and continued to cover operations on the North African coast from the vicinity of the Balearic Islands.

During January 1943, the *Furious*, with Force H, covered Mediterranean convoys to Algiers; in February she returned to the Home Fleet with which she operated for the rest of her active service. On the 7th July, the *Furious*, with other units of the Home Fleet, left Scapa Flow for a demonstration of force off the coast of Norway. This operation was made to distract the enemy and pin down his forces during the invasion of Sicily which was about to begin. The Fleet returned on the 9th July without incident, except that a German reconnaissance aircraft—after deliberately being allowed to make a sighting report of our forces—was destroyed by Martlet fighters from the carrier.

In 1944 the *Furious* participated in several anti-shipping strikes off Norway with the Home Fleet; these included two major attacks against the German Battleship *Tirpitz*, with Barracuda aircraft, sheltering in Norwegian Fjords. Her last operation was in September when she took part in an air mining operation near Norway; on her return she was placed in the Reserve Fleet. A special signal was sent to the C.in.C. Home Fleet by the Admiralty recalling the great services that she had performed almost continuously for more than a quarter of a century. After serving as an accommodation ship for a few years she was sold for breaking up in February 1948; she was finally berthed at Gareloch in the Clyde.

LEADING PARTICULARS
Displacement: 22,450 tons.
Dimensions: $786\frac{1}{2}$ ft. O.A.; $89\frac{3}{4}$ ft. (including bulges).
Machinery: Geared Turbines, 90,000 S.H.P.; Speed, 31 knots.
Armament: (Final) 12 4·5-in. D.P. 3 Multiple Pom-Poms. Several 20 m.m.
Aircraft: (Final), about 33. Complement: about 1,200.

(Imperial War Museum photo)

Vindictive after re-conversion

Vindictive   1917

THE *Vindictive*, although she contributed virtually nothing to naval aviation, had an extremely chequered career. Originally she had been laid down as the cruiser *Cavendish* but, during the course of her construction, it was decided to change her name and convert her into a carrier. When completed she looked something like a smaller edition of the *Furious*, except that she had two funnels. As well as the, by now, normal flying-off deck forward, she had a landing deck aft of about 200 ft. in length; both decks were linked by a bridge, on the port side, at the same level as the decks. Underneath these decks were hangars and a lift was fitted towards the rear of the forward deck.

All in all it seemed like a good design as the time of her commissioning drew near. However, on board the *Furious*, deck landing trials were

Vindictive   (*Imperial War Museum photo*)

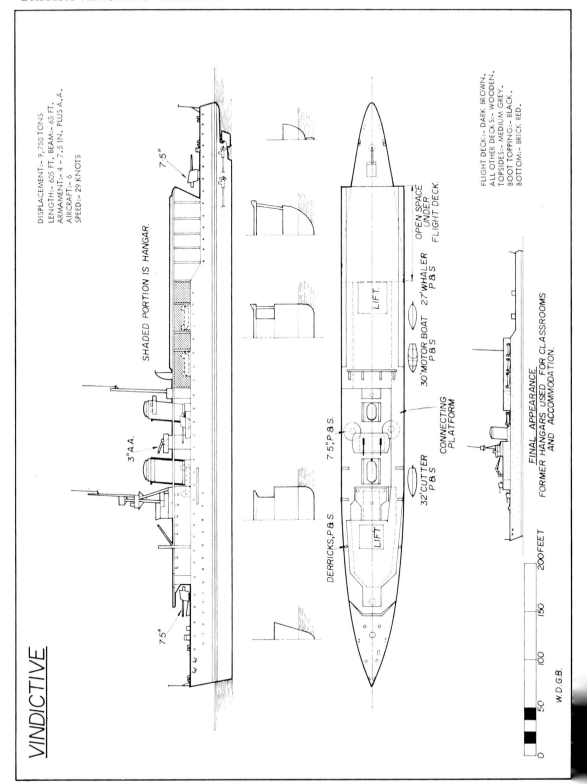

VINDICTIVE

DISPLACEMENT:- 9,750 TONS
LENGTH:- 605 FT. BEAM:- 65 FT.
ARMAMENT:- 4 – 7.5 IN. PLUS A.A.
AIRCRAFT:- 6
SPEED:- 29 KNOTS

SHADED PORTION IS HANGAR.

7.5"

3" A.A.

7.5"

OPEN SPACE UNDER FLIGHT DECK.

27' WHALER P & S

30' MOTOR BOAT P & S

CONNECTING PLATFORM

32' CUTTER P & S

7.5", P & S.

LIFT.

DERRICKS, P & S.

LIFT.

FLIGHT DECK:- DARK BROWN.
ALL OTHER DECKS:- WOODEN.
TOPSIDES:- MEDIUM GREY.
BOOT TOPPING:- BLACK.
BOTTOM:- BRICK RED.

FINAL APPEARANCE
FORMER HANGARS USED FOR CLASSROOMS AND ACCOMMODATION.

0 50 100 150 200 FEET

W.D.G.B.

c

going very badly; after Squadron Commander Dunning's tragic second landing attempt there followed several other bad crashes, and the Navy was learning—the hard way—that a short obstructed landing deck was not the answer to the problem. These setbacks caused the re-construction of the *Furious* to be put in abeyance, and this deferment consequently affected all the other carriers or part carriers then building. Only one landing on the deck of the *Vindictive* was ever attempted before experiments were stopped on account of the experience gained from the *Furious*.

For the last month of the war the *Vindictive* operated with the fleet as a seaplane carrier and then she was placed in the Reserve Fleet until 1925. In that year she emerged for a short while as a seaplane carrier but, like all ships of that type, she had only a very limited operational capability; the subsequent design of aircraft carriers had overtaken her. Compared with the larger carrier conversions — *Furious, Eagle, Glorious* and *Courageous*—she was too light a ship to build on the considerable topworks required for a really successful carrier. Therefore it was decided to convert her back into a cruiser again.

During the conversion that followed, it was decided to retain the forward hangar and the existing armament of 7·5 in. guns; this was never a popular type of gun with the Navy; although it fired a heavier shell than the more common 6 in., its range was not a lot longer and its rate of fire was much slower, neither did it compare with the 8 in. gun mounted in heavy cruisers of that period. The *Vindictive* and her two sister ships were the only cruisers to retain this calibre.

From 1936 to 1937 yet another big conversion was carried out. This time she was altered into a cadets' training ship and, in the process, her rear funnel was discarded. A training armament of 4·7 in. guns was fitted, provision was made for class rooms and extra accommodation; her former hangar was to prove extremely useful in this respect.

Her career as a training ship ended with the outbreak of the Second World War; cadets did not go to sea any more for their training, which was now carried out ashore. Once again it was decided to carry out another conversion—this time she was converted into a repair ship. In this role she carried out very useful work throughout the war. Shortly after the end of the war, February 1946, she was scrapped at Blyth; it is very doubtful if there has ever been a warship, of any nation, that has had such a record number of conversions.

LEADING PARTICULARS
Displacement: 9,750 tons.
Length: 605 ft. Beam: 65 ft.
Machinery: Geared Turbines; 60,000 S.H.P. Speed: 29 knots (as a training ship S.H.P. and speed considerably reduced).
Armament: (as a carrier), four 7·5 in.; four 3 in. A.A.; four 12pdr.
Aircraft: Six.
Complement: 730.

H.M.S. Argus

Argus 1918

THE *Argus* was the first ship of the Royal Navy to have been designed as an aircraft carrier, as the earlier ships had all been improvised from other types. In 1916 authority was given for an aircraft carrier to be built in accordance with plans originally prepared before the First World War by Messrs. Beardmore and an Admiralty Committee, and later modified as a result of the experience that had been gained.

To save time the partly built hull of an Italian passenger liner—the *Conte Rosso*, destined for the Lloyd Sabaudo Line—on which no work had been done since 1914, was taken over. Fortunately it was lying at the Beardmore yard at Balmuir and so this company was able to put into practice their plans drawn up over two years before. Just before the war ended, September 1918, the ship, renamed *Argus*, was completed. In appearance she was quite unique, having a completely unobstructed flight deck overall— this was to earn her the nickname 'Flat Iron' later, and a glance at the plan view of this ship will suffice to show why. The charthouse was provided with a hydraulic lift and horizontal smoke ducts—with big fans—expelled the furnace gases and smoke out over the stern.

With only two months of the war to run, the *Argus* joined the Grand Fleet, but there were no actions for her to participate in. When the Grand Fleet dispersed in April 1919, she served with the Atlantic Fleet. (It may be of interest to note that the present-day Home Fleet was called the Atlantic Fleet and previous to this was called the Channel Fleet; the Grand Fleet was the name given in the 1914 to 1918 war to the huge British Fleet that was assembled in Home Waters during this period).

During 1925 to 1926 she was refitted and her anti-torpedo bulges were fitted, and for the next 11 years she continued giving valuable service and experience with the Atlantic and Home Fleets. In 1937 she was again taken in hand for re-fitting; modifications were incorporated so that she could act as a tender for 'Queen Bee' pilotless aircraft and, also, serve as a general anti-aircraft target service ship. (The 'Queen Bee' was a Tiger Moth fitted with a comprehensive radio set that enabled the aircraft to be remotely controlled; it was usually fitted with floats). When the Second World War broke out she was being employed on these training duties and based at Portsmouth.

Alterations were made at this stage to fit her for duty as a deck landing training carrier and on their completion in the November she proceeded to the Mediterranean. For some time she was based at Toulon; however, after the entry of Italy into the war and the collapse of France in June 1940 she returned to the Clyde.

A couple of months later the *Argus* was under way again to the Mediterranean. This time she took part in the first of a long series of operations whereby aircraft to reinforce Malta were flown there from carriers in the Western Mediterranean. She was also used to carry fighter aircraft to Takoradi, on the Gold Coast, from whence they were flown across Africa to Egypt. Her first visit to this port was on the 5th September, 1940, and on the way she also acted as escort for a troopship convoy—bound for the Middle East—as far as Freetown.

In November she carried out a second aircraft ferrying operation to Malta; this time the operation was to be marred with tragedy. Eight out of the 12 Hurricanes ran out of fuel and were lost at sea; it was considered that the pilots had not received adequate training with regard to the range and endurance of their aircraft. The next month the *Argus* left the Clyde as part of the escort of a Middle East Troop convoy; this convoy was attacked by the German cruiser *Admiral Hipper* on Christmas morning and one transport was slightly damaged. Poor visibility prevented the carrier from flying off her aircraft to hunt down the intruder, however. She accompanied the convoy as far as Gibraltar and returned to the Clyde in January 1941.

Nineteen forty-one was to be another busy year for the ship. In March and April she again ferried fighter aircraft to Gibraltar from whence they were taken by the *Ark Royal* to Malta. Another Middle East troop convoy was escorted in May on the first stage of its long voyage round the Cape of Good Hope. After this escort duty the *Argus* resumed deck landing training in the Clyde; this, however, was not for long.

As part of the first convoy sent to North Russia, in August 1941, she carried there a

ARGUS

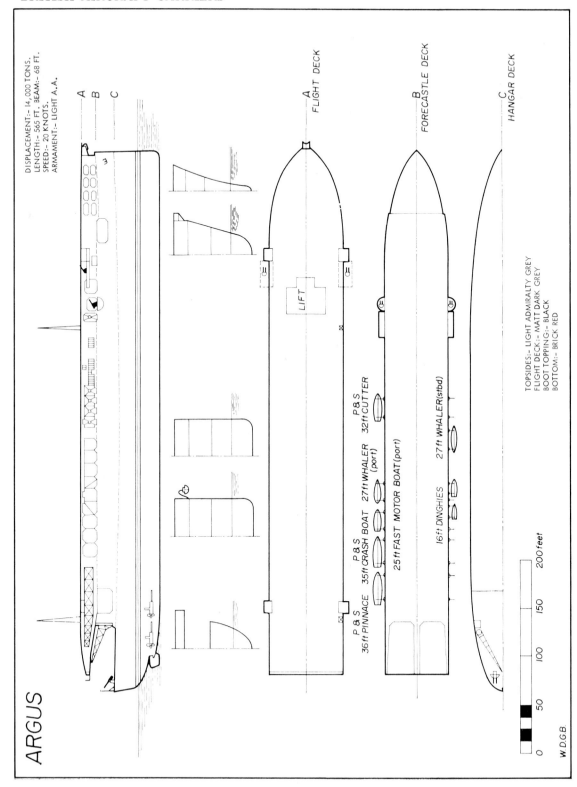

DISPLACEMENT:- 14,000 TONS.
LENGTH:- 565 FT. BEAM:- 68 FT.
SPEED:- 20 KNOTS.
ARMAMENT:- LIGHT A.A.

A
B
C

A
FLIGHT DECK

B
FORECASTLE DECK

C
HANGAR DECK

LIFT

P & S
32ft CUTTER

P & S
27ft WHALER
(port)

25ft FAST MOTOR BOAT (port)

P & S
35ft CRASH BOAT

P & S
36ft PINNACE

16ft DINGHIES

27ft WHALER (stbd)

TOPSIDES:- LIGHT ADMIRALTY GREY
FLIGHT DECK:- MATT DARK GREY
BOOT TOPPING:- BLACK
BOTTOM:- BRICK RED

0   50   100   150   200 feet

W.D.G.B.

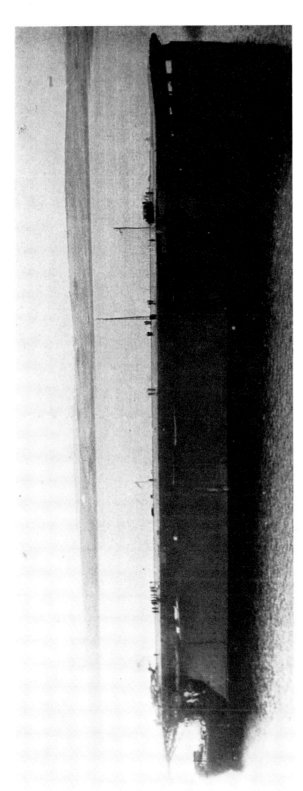

squadron of R.A.F. Hurricanes; these were flown off in the Murmansk area on the 7th September. This first ever convoy to Russia was called, appropriately, Operation 'Benedict'.

During October and November she made further passages to Gibraltar with more aircraft to be ferried on to Malta. It was during the November operation that the *Ark Royal*, whilst returning to Gibraltar and not far from there, was sunk by a German submarine; the *Argus* was retained in Force H to take her place for a while.

For the first six months of 1942 she took part in several more operations for the ferrying of aircraft into Malta and escorting convoys to the island. Then she returned home to resume her role of training carrier, and during the September she had a minor refit in the Tyne. By November 1942, however, she was back in the Western Mediterranean for the landings in North Africa – Operation 'Torch'.

Whilst operating off Algiers, on the 10th November, she was damaged by a direct hit and several near misses from enemy aircraft; this put her out of action for a month. On the 11th December the *Argus* left the Clyde as senior officer's ship in the escort of a large North African troop convoy, and she arrived back in the Clyde on the 31st December.

The new year began in the same way as the old one ended, and once again she acted as the senior officer's ship for a North Africa-bound convoy. On the way back home she escorted a returning convoy and arrived in the Clyde on the 9th February. There she was taken in hand for repairs (her earlier repairs were only temporary) until the end of April.

From May 1943, she reverted to her former and what was supposed to be primary role of deck landing training carrier until August 1944. At this time there were plenty of carriers in the service to take the burden off this, by now, weary old veteran. When the war ended she was employed as an accommodation ship at Chatham Dockyard. For two years she served in this quiet role before making her last voyage, March, 1947, to the scrapyard at Inverkeithing.

LEADING PARTICULARS

Displacement: 14,000 tons.

Length: 565 ft. Beam (excluding bulges): 68 ft.

Machinery: Turbines, 20,000 S.H.P. Speed: 20 knots.

Armament: Several small A.A. guns.

Complement: 373 (excluding air personnel).

Aircraft: Varying numbers according to role.

H.M.S. Eagle *(Imperial War Museum photo)*

Eagle

1920

BEFORE the First World War the battleship represented the ultimate in terms of a deterrent. Many South American countries acquired, or were acquiring, these expensive items for their armouries from Britain and the U.S.A.; Argentina at one time was spending 25 per cent of her total income, to the exclusion of all else, on battleships. This then was the background when, in 1913, Chile ordered two large battleships from Britain.

The two ships were to be named the *Almirante Cochrane* and the *Almirante Latorre*, after the heroes of the war of independence with Spain in the early nineteenth century. With a main armament of ten 14-in. guns, mounted in five turrets of two guns each, they would have been an extremely formidable addition to the Chilean Navy.

When the First World War started both ships were acquired by the Royal Navy for the duration. The *Almirante Latorre* was renamed *Canada* and completed in time to take part in the Battle of Jutland; in 1920 she was returned to Chile and was in service until the late 'fifties.

Eagle

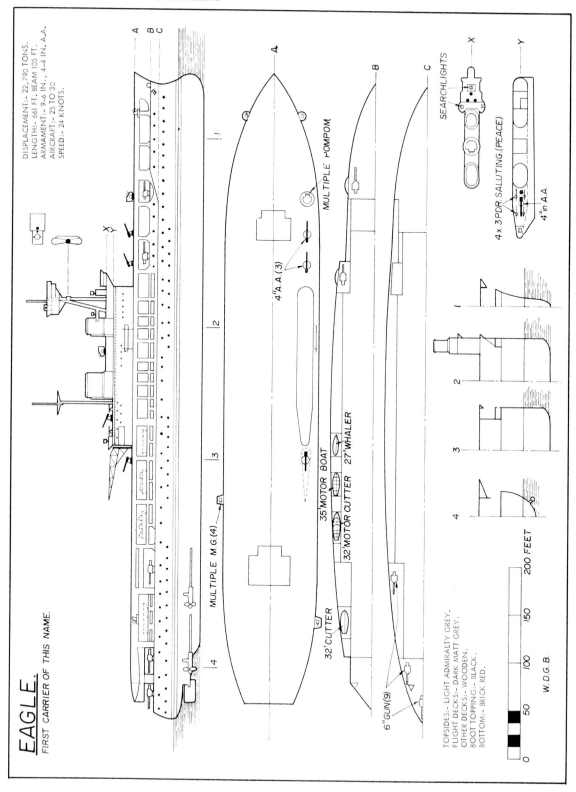

EAGLE.
FIRST CARRIER OF THIS NAME.

DISPLACEMENT:- 22,790 TONS.
LENGTH:- 661 FT. BEAM 105 FT.
ARMAMENT:- 9·6 IN., 4·4 IN. A.A.
AIRCRAFT:- 25 TO 30
SPEED:- 24 KNOTS.

MULTIPLE POMPOM

4" A.A. (3)

MULTIPLE M.G.(4)

35' MOTOR BOAT   27' WHALER
32' MOTOR CUTTER

32' CUTTER

6" GUN (9)

SEARCHLIGHTS

X

4 x 3 PDR. SALUTING (PEACE)
4" in A.A.

Y

TOPSIDES:- LIGHT ADMIRALTY GREY.
FLIGHT DECKS:- DARK MATT GREY.
OTHER DECKS:- WOODEN.
BOOT TOPPING:- BLACK.
BOTTOM:- BRICK RED.

0   50   100   150   200 FEET
W.D.G.B.

agle

Her sister ship's career, the *Almirante Cochrane*, was destined to be very different. In 1917 she was purchased outright by the Admiralty, who had earmarked her for conversion to an aircraft carrier, and renamed *Eagle*.

During the re-construction that followed the principle, learnt by bitter experience in the *Furious*, of a clear, unobstructed flight deck was paramount. However, as mentioned earlier, the constructors had to retain the funnel trunkings and—from the naval point of view—it was considered desirable to steer and control a ship of this type from the conventional bridge. In the event, after trials carried out in the *Argus* with a dummy superstructure, a practical compromise was reached with the funnels, bridge and superstructure well over on the starboard side. When she emerged fully completed, in 1924, she had a very distinctive appearance as the only two funnelled carrier in the world.

The first seven years of her life, with the exception of refits, were spent in the Mediterranean; a brief description of life in the peacetime Mediterranean is given in the chapter on the *Courageous* and *Glorious*. During 1932 to 1933 she underwent modernisation at Devonport and, when this was completed, she went to the China station for two years. In 1936 to 1937 she was back at Devonport but returned to the Far East the following year.

When the Second World War started she was at Singapore but was soon under way; in October 1939, she was part of Force I hunting for the *Graf Spee* in the Indian Ocean. For the first two months of 1940 she was escorting troop convoys from Australia to the Middle East. On the 14th March she was damaged by an internal explosion in her forward bomb room, in which 13 ratings were killed, and she returned to Singapore for repairs.

In May 1940, she joined the Mediterranean Fleet and on the 5th July her aircraft attacked enemy shipping in Tobruk harbour. They sank the Italian destroyer *Zeffiro*, two merchant ships, and badly damaged a large troop transport which had to be scuttled later. Four days later she was in action again off Calabria when her aircraft attacked the Italian Fleet but without result. During her return to Alexandria, after this engagement, she was heavily bombed and had several near misses; four Italian bombers were shot down during these attacks.

Less than two weeks later, on the 20th July, her aircraft were back in action with another raid on Tobruk. This time they sank two more destroyers, the *Ostro* and *Nembo*, and another merchant ship. On the 22nd August her aircraft

43

(Imperial War Museum photo)

Eagle

attacked and sank the Italian submarine *Iride* in the Gulf of Bomba; at the end of the month her aircraft attacked the airfield at Maritza in Rhodes. For the next six months she provided cover for convoys in the Eastern Mediterranean and, during this period, her aircraft attacked Italian airfields and shipping and laid mines. On the 11th November some of her aircraft were embarked in the *Illustrious* and took part in the Taranto raid.

In March 1941, she was ordered through the Suez canal but her passage was delayed on account of a wreck in the canal. However, her aircraft were flown on to Port Sudan and assisted in the destruction of Italian ships at Massawa and in the Red Sea. After eventually passing through the canal she arrived at Simonstown on the 8th May; from there she went round Africa to Freetown and remained on the South Atlantic station until October.

Apart from routine convoy escort duties she took part in operations which led to the sinking and capture of German ships. These were the *Elbe* on the 6th June, which her aircraft attacked and sunk, and the *Lothringen*—in conjunction with the cruiser *Dunedin*—which was intercepted and surrendered. Both these successes were in mid-Atlantic, about 1,000 miles west of the Cape Verde Islands.

A short time was spent in the U.K., refitting, and in February 1942, the *Eagle* left again for the Mediterranean. She took part in several Malta convoys carrying aircraft for the R.A.F. there and also providing fighter cover. On the 11th August, 1942, while escorting a convoy to Malta (Operation Pedestal), she was hit by four torpedoes from the German submarine U.73 and sank within 10 minutes; 927 of her ship's company were picked up, including her captain, but 160 did not survive, unfortunately. Those of her fighters in the air, at the time, landed on the *Victorious* and *Formidable* and carried on the fight from these ships.

LEADING PARTICULARS
Displacement: 22,790 tons.
Length: 661 ft. Beam: 105 ft.
Machinery: Turbines 37,000 S.H.P. Speed 24 knots.
Armament: Nine 6 in.; four 4 in. A.A.; seven 2pdr. A.A.
Aircraft: 25 to 30.
Complement: About 1,200.

Hermes

1923

BY the beginning of 1918 the usefulness of the aircraft carrier was more fully appreciated by the Royal Navy; the earlier carriers had and were pioneering the idea and way of naval aviation. In the January of that year a historic event took place; the first ship in the world ever to be designed from the keel up as an aircraft carrier was laid down—the *Hermes*. Construction, pressed by urgent wartime requirements, was initially comparatively fast, and she was launched in the September of the following year.

However, with the war over and with the experiments being carried out in the *Furious*, further construction was delayed and more leisurely. In 1920 she was towed from the Vickers Armstrong yard to Devonport and finally completed in 1923. Like the *Eagle*, her superstructure and funnel were placed on the starboard side, giving a clear flight deck. Displacing around 10,000 tons, she was very much smaller than the other contemporary

Hermes

HERMES.

FIRST AIRCRAFT CARRIER OF THIS NAME.

NOTE DISTINCT HUMP AT STERN.

DISPLACEMENT:- 10,850 TONS.
LENGTH:- 600 FT. BEAM:- 90FT.
ARMAMENT:- 6–5.5 IN., 3–4 IN. A.A.
AIRCRAFT:- 15.
SPEED:- 24 KNOTS (APPROX).

CONTROL TOWER

CALCULATING
POSITION

RANGE
FINDER

RANGE FINDERS, P & S.

C
D

A
B

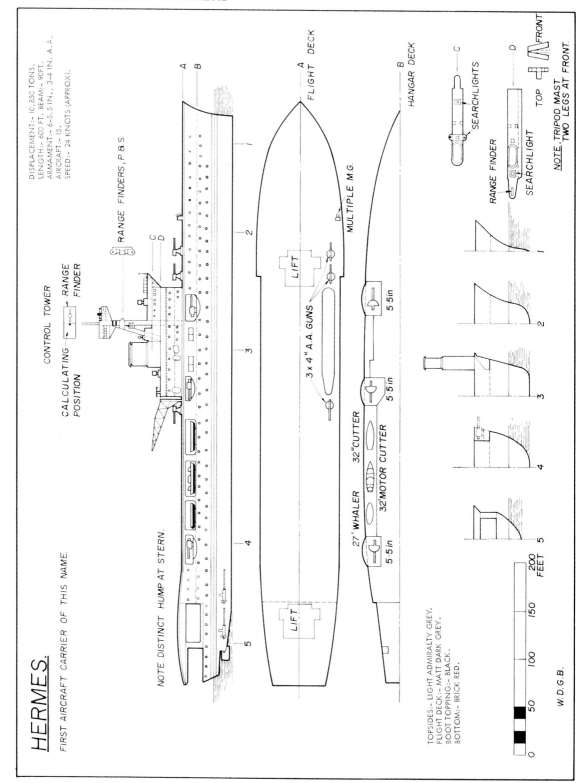

A
FLIGHT DECK

LIFT

MULTIPLE M.G.

3 x 4" A.A. GUNS

5.5 in

5.5 in

27' WHALER

32" CUTTER

32' MOTOR CUTTER

5.5 in

HANGAR DECK

B

I

2

3

4

5

RANGE FINDER

SEARCHLIGHTS

SEARCHLIGHT

C

D

TOP

FRONT

NOTE, TRIPOD MAST
TWO LEGS AT FRONT.

2

3

4

5

TOPSIDES:- LIGHT ADMIRALTY GREY.
FLIGHT DECK:- MATT DARK GREY.
BOOT TOPPING:- BLACK.
BOTTOM:- BRICK RED.

0   50   100   150   200
FEET

W.D.G.B.

46

Hermes

carriers, having, in consequence, a much lower freeboard and shallower draught. Her hangar was small and could only accommodate up to 15 aircraft; taking everything into account, her design, although original and on the right lines, was not a great success, too much having been attempted on too little.

The years before the Second World War were spent mainly in the Far East, alternating with the *Eagle*. Although she was a handy little ship—in many ways she had the characteristics, and certainly must have been the forerunner, of the light fleet carriers of later years—she was too small and too slow to operate with the Home and Mediterranean Fleets. With only 12 to 15 aircraft of various types she could not provide adequate fighter protection nor could she provide a strong striking force.

When the war broke out the *Hermes* was in the U.K. after a spell of duty in the Far East. Much of the first year of the war was spent searching the Atlantic, in company with other warships, for German raiders. After most of the raiders had been hunted down, or accounted for, she joined the South Atlantic hunting group, covering convoys.

In June 1940, after the fall of France, she kept watch on the French Fleet at Dakar, West Africa; the most powerful unit of this fleet was the new battleship *Richelieu*. On the 8th July one of *Hermes*' motor boats, under the command of Lieutenant Commander R. N. Bristowe, succeeded in getting through the harbour boom and dropped four depth charges under the stern of the *Richelieu*. The motor boat made good her escape and, after 15 hours, was hoisted on board the carrier again. Unfortunately none of the depth charges exploded due to the shallowness of the water; in the event the French Fleet remained neutral and later on, in the Pacific, the *Richelieu* did good work for the Allies.

Two days after this incident the British force was withdrawn from the area but, during the night of the 10th July, in a sudden dense tropical storm, the *Hermes* collided with the armed merchant cruiser *Corfu*. She suffered severe damage to her bows and the fore-end of her flight deck; however, she managed to reach Freetown that evening under her own steam. The following month she went to Simonstown for a refit which lasted until November.

Early in 1941 the offensive against Italian East Africa began and the *Hermes* did good work there. Her aircraft spotted for the bombarding warships' guns and carried out photographic reconnaissance flights. Between the 10th and 19th February her Swordfish intercepted and forced several enemy supply ships towards a British cruiser—*Hawkins*, a sister ship of the early carrier *Vindictive*—which, in turn, put armed guards on board. Previously prepared directions, in German and Italian, contained in bags, were dropped by the Swordfish on to the decks of the ships. One German ship was abandoned by her crew on being sighted by one of the carrier's aircraft; another, carrying troops, was bombed and damaged. Only one enemy supply ship escaped through the web woven by the carrier; this action was a classical example of the value of a small carrier in a limited war.

Towards the end of April 1941, the *Hermes* was recalled from the Indian Ocean, where she had been employed hunting for enemy shipping, to patrol the Persian Gulf. German activities in Iraq forced the British to intervene and, although this was almost entirely a land campaign, some part was played by aircraft from the carrier.

Six of her Swordfish made demonstration flights over Basra on the 3rd and 7th May. Owing to the distance of the ship from the sphere of action a small striking force was based ashore at the R.A.F. base of Shaibah. Between the 4th and 16th May, 10 dive bombing attacks were made on railway bridges, petrol and oil tanks, barracks and troop concentrations. Several aircraft were hit by the extremely accurate rifle and automatic fire of the Iraqi irregulars. One Swordfish was forced down and was immediately surrounded by the Iraqis who opened fire as they approached the aircraft. Another pilot, Lieutenant Dundas, landed his Swordfish alongside and—under heavy fire and

on rough terrain—rescued the other crew and took off again for base.

From May until November the *Hermes* continued to be employed on trade protection, convoy escort, and the interception of enemy shipping in the Indian Ocean. After a refit at Simonstown she left there on the 2nd January, 1942, being attached to the Australian Squadron for operations in the Anzac area. She returned to the East Indies in February and was temporarily retained in the Colombo area while the *Indomitable* was ferrying aircraft to the Far East.

At the beginning of April reports were received of an imminent Japanese air attack on Ceylon so, on the night of the 8th, it was decided to clear Trincomalee harbour. The *Hermes* and the *Vampire*, an Australian destroyer of World War One vintage, were ordered to sail to the southward so as to be at least 40 miles from the harbour by dawn the next day. Unfortunately they were sighted by an enemy reconnaissance aircraft and at dawn on the 9th they were attacked by some 50 Japanese carrier-based aircraft. Completely overwhelmed, they were sunk off Batticaloa; just over three hundred of her ship's company, including her captain, went down with her.

Displacement: 10,850 tons.
Length: 600 ft. Beam: 90 ft.
Machinery: Geared Turbines; Speed 24 knots (approx.).
Armament: Six 5·5 in.; three 4 in. A.A.
Aircraft: 15.
Complement: 750 (approx.).

Courageous and
Glorious   1925

SURPRISINGLY enough the story of these two ships, along with the *Furious*, began as long ago as 1907. Plans were made around then for the capture of Borkum, or one of the other Frisian Islands, to use as a base for the penetration of the Baltic. Such a scheme, if successful, with the early Russian advance into Eastern Germany in 1914, would have led to a link-up with the Russians.

Specially designed for this operation, these ships had a comparatively shallow draught of 25 ft., as opposed to the 30 ft. plus of conventional battle cruisers, which could be reduced to 22 ft. This, of course, was essential for operating in the shallow waters around the Frisian Islands. A main armament of four 15-in. guns, mounted in two turrets of two guns, was carried; a strong secondary battery included 18 4-in. guns and, in addition, there were 14 torpedo tubes. By the time these two ships were completed, the end of 1916, the plans for the original operation had been shelved. These large lightly armed and armoured ships became 'white elephants'; they could not be fitted into normal fleet operations, and spent most of the war in a reserve capacity.

For a few years after the war they retained their original status of light battle cruisers then, in the early 'twenties, it was decided to convert them into aircraft carriers. As they were very similar to the *Furious* the conversion was carried out on the lines of this ship. When completed— the *Courageous* was the first to join the fleet in 1925, and the *Glorious* followed nearly two years later—they strongly resembled the *Furious*. However, after the experience gained with the *Eagle* and *Hermes*, they both retained their funnels in a small bridge superstructure on the starboard side. The main visible differences between the two ships were:—

(1) The *Glorious* had a slightly longer flight deck in the form of an overhang at the stern.

(2) The quarterdeck of the *Glorious* was one deck higher than that of the *Courageous*.

Both these points are shown clearly in the photographs.

The peace-time career of the *Courageous* was spent with the Atlantic and Home Fleets; generally speaking, the Fleet followed a fairly set routine. In January it would cruise to Gibraltar and, from there, went on to Malta for rendezvous and exercises with the Mediterranean Fleet; some years it went to the Canary Islands as well. At the end of March they returned to U.K. for, usually, a period of intensive activity in preparation for the summer cruises. On the first summer cruise they ranged the coasts of Britain, with occasional courtesy visits to European ports, up to Scarborough and Rosyth. The second summer cruise was to Scapa Flow and more operational type exercises were carried out this time. In the autumn they would cruise off the North West coast of Scotland before returning to their permanent bases —Portsmouth, Plymouth and Chatham—in preparation for the cruise to Gibraltar in January.

Most of the peace-time career of the *Glorious* was spent with the Mediterranean Fleet; hers was a much more attractive way of life. After the rendezvous with the Home Fleet, in January, the Western Mediterranean was toured; such enchanting places as the French and Italian Rivieras would be visited. July and August, the hot months of the Mediterranean, would be spent in the vicinity of Malta. Following these months came the first autumn cruise going up the Adriatic coast calling in at Corfu, Spoleto, Caltaro, Venice and Trieste. After this another short period was spent in Malta before commencing the second autumn cruise. This time the Fleet went eastwards to Crete, Cyprus, Alexandria, the Greek Islands, and the Aegean Sea. With the mild winter approaching they

D

H.M.S. Courageous

H.M.S. "Courageous"

50

D*

H.M.S. "Glorious" 1935.

H.M.S. Glorious

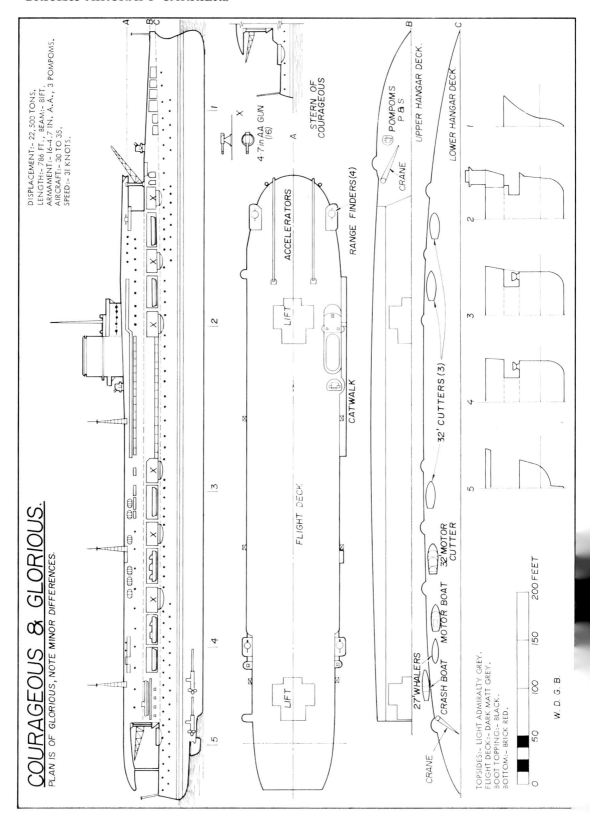

COURAGEOUS & GLORIOUS.

PLAN IS OF GLORIOUS, NOTE MINOR DIFFERENCES.

DISPLACEMENT:- 22,500 TONS.
LENGTH:- 786 FT., BEAM:- 81FT.
ARMAMENT:- 16-4.7 IN., A.A., 3 POMPOMS.
AIRCRAFT:- 30 TO 35.
SPEED:- 31 KNOTS.

4.7 in AA GUN (6)

STERN OF COURAGEOUS

A B C

ACCELERATORS

RANGE FINDERS (4)

LIFT

CATWALK

FLIGHT DECK

LIFT

POMPOMS P & S

CRANE

UPPER HANGAR DECK.

LOWER HANGAR DECK

27 WHALERS

CRASH BOAT

MOTOR BOAT

32' MOTOR CUTTER

32' CUTTERS (3)

CRANE

TOPSIDES:- LIGHT ADMIRALTY GREY.
FLIGHT DECK:- DARK MATT GREY.
BOOT TOPPING:- BLACK.
BOTTOM:- BRICK RED.

0   50   100   150   200 FEET

W. D. G. B.

returned to Malta for exercises and preparations were made for the January rendezvous with the Home Fleet.

It was not all 'beer and skittles' for the aircraft carriers though. A great deal of flying took place and experiments were made including night flying—at that time, with no arrester hooks and wires, this was a dangerous business, to say the least. Accidents were frequent and many lives were lost, but gradually, as experience was gained, techniques were established that bore fruit in the war that was approaching. On board the *Glorious* was born the idea and, more important, the practical plans were made, for the famous attack on the Italian Fleet at Taranto some years later.

Fourteen days after the Second World War started the *Courageous*, on an anti-submarine sweep with four destroyers, was torpedoed and sunk by a German submarine. Fortunately, there was not a great loss of life but her destruction, at this very early state of the war, was a heavy blow to the entirely inadequate and widely dispersed carrier force of the Royal Navy.

With the loss of the *Courageous*, the *Glorious* came home to replace her in the Home Fleet. Her early war days were not very hectic, in common with most of the larger warships, and routine anti-submarine sweeps and patrols were carried out. Then came the Norwegian campaign, commencing in April 1940. The work of the carriers changed overnight from their unspectacular role of submarine hunting to offensive operations in support of the Norwegian Expeditionary Force.

The distance from U.K. bases made it impossible for the R.A.F. to provide fighter protection until aerodromes in Norway had been prepared; the brunt of the air defence fell on the carrier-borne fighters. (At the present time the same sort of situation could so easily come about; with modern jet fighters requiring runways and sophisticated bases the position would be even more aggravated—if our commitments remain the same, lack of carriers could be extremely embarrassing, to say the least). Within one hundred miles of the coast, sailing in very dangerous waters, the carriers were there in the background, watchful and vigilant. Their aircraft flew in appalling weather and opposed an enemy that was superior both in numbers and performance.

On the 24th April the *Glorious*, with the *Ark Royal*, arrived off the Norwegian coast. She carried a Skua and Gladiator squadron of her own and, in addition, an R.A.F. Gladiator squadron which was flown off to operate from a

Glorious

frozen lake. For the next four days the carrier aircraft flew intensively on patrols over convoys and coastal areas in the neighbourhood of Namsos and Aandalsnes; they also made raids on ships and seaplanes in Trondheim harbour and on land targets. Nine seaplanes were sunk, two tankers were set on fire and four aircraft hangars were destroyed. As a result of the many air combats, 20 enemy aircraft were shot down and at least another 20 were badly damaged; sometimes these air combats were fought at odds of six to one.

After a brief respite, the two carriers continued their operations in the Narvik area. Towards the end of May the *Glorious* returned to U.K. to transport R.A.F. fighters – Hurricanes and Gladiators – back to the newly completed air-fields in Norway.

At the beginning of June the evacuation from Norway commenced. The *Glorious* re-embarked the surviving R.A.F. Hurricanes—neither the Hurricanes, nor their pilots, had ever made deck landings before; it is to their eternal credit that all of them landed on safely. When the re-embarkation was completed, the carrier was detached back to the U.K. with only two destroyers, all that could be spared, for an escort.

On the way home she was intercepted by the German battle cruisers *Scharnhorst* and *Gneisenau*. In the appalling weather that prevailed and with an overcrowded flight deck the carrier had no chance; with her gallant little escorts she fought to the last, but within forty minutes all three were sunk. Tragically there were less than forty survivors.

LEADING PARTICULARS
Displacement: 22,500 tons.
Dimensions: Length, 786 ft. Beam, 81 ft.
Machinery: Geared Turbines, 90,000 S.H.P. Speed: 31 to 33 knots.
Armament: 16 4·7 in. A.A.
Aircraft: About 30 to 35.
Complement: 1,216.

Albatross
1928

BY 1928 the aircraft carrier was well established in its basic design; it might seem, at the first glance, that a retrograde step had been taken when a seaplane carrier emerged at this time. The small, but efficient, Australian Navy had recognised the growing importance of naval aviation long before the Second World War. However, they could not afford to own an aircraft carrier in the 'twenties; even if they could have afforded one, they simply did not have anywhere near enough the personnel to man it. This then was the background to the Australian-built *Albatross*.

When completed, the ship was a far cry from the early seaplane carriers of the First World War. The forward two-thirds of the ship was almost entirely devoted to the carriage and handling of seaplanes; the rear third contained the machinery, bridge, accommodation and boats. Her hangar could take nine aircraft, a catapult was fitted in the bows and three workmanlike cranes, strategically positioned, handled the aircraft with ease. For a small ship she was given a reasonable armament and a fair turn of speed—21 knots; no one could ever claim that she was the last word in naval aviation but, all the same, she was an interesting and effective compromise and deserves mentioning.

With the arrival of three modern cruisers nearly ten years later, each equipped with their own aircraft, there was no longer any requirement for the *Albatross* to remain with the Australian Fleet. So, in 1938, she was purchased by Britain and joined the Royal Navy. As most of the British capital ships and cruisers carried their own seaplanes, it was not too apparent, at that time, just how this seaplane carrier was going to fit in with the fleet. However, within a year of her acquisition, the Second World War commenced and the little ship was certainly going to justify herself.

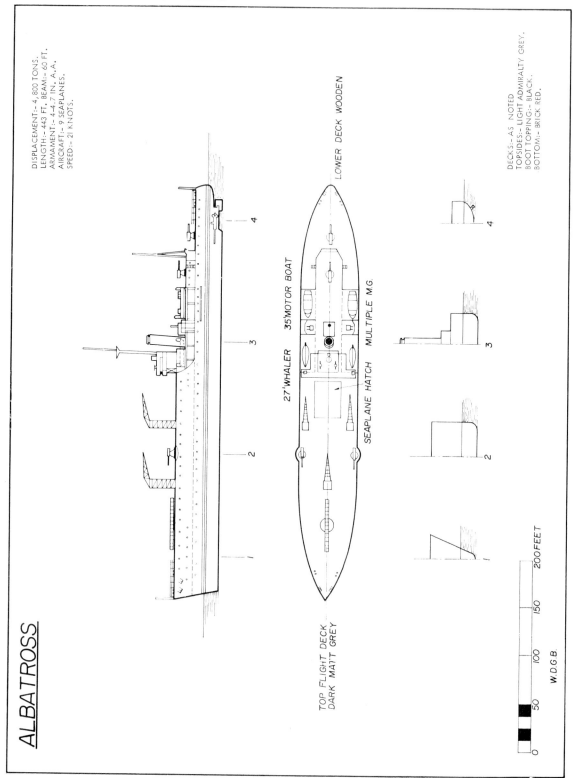

ALBATROSS

DISPLACEMENT:- 4,800 TONS.
LENGTH:- 443 FT. BEAM:- 60 FT.
ARMAMENT:- 4-4.7 IN, A.A.
AIRCRAFT:- 9 SEAPLANES.
SPEED:- 21 KNOTS.

LOWER DECK WOODEN

35 MOTOR BOAT

27' WHALER

MULTIPLE M.G.

SEAPLANE HATCH

TOP FLIGHT DECK
DARK MATT GREY

DECKS:- AS NOTED
TOPSIDES:- LIGHT ADMIRALTY GREY.
BOOT TOPPING:- BLACK.
BOTTOM:- BRICK RED.

W.D.G.B.

0   50   100   150   200 FEET

56

After the loss of the *Courageous* and *Glorious* the Navy was extremely short of air power at sea for quite a while; the *Albatross* filled a useful gap. Operating in the South Atlantic, mostly from the Freetown area in West Africa, her Walrus aircraft—a small, amphibian biplane flying boat with a crew of three—escorted convoys along that stretch of the coast. In addition they carried out intensive anti-submarine patrol work and air sea rescue duties in the general area. As the war progressed her usefulness in this role declined with the introduction and growth of the escort carrier; these ships, apart from carrying better-equipped aircraft for anti-submarine duties, were able to sail and operate with the convoys, which was a far more satisfactory arrangement.

As a result it was decided, in 1942, to convert the seaplane carrier into a repair ship; with her hangar space and cranes she was ideally suited for this change of role. After her conversion, the *Albatross* joined the Eastern Fleet and carried out useful but unspectacular service for over a year. Towards the end of 1943 she returned to the U.K. again in preparation for the invasion of Europe. She took part in the Normandy landings but, as damage to the participating ships was much lighter than expected, her specialist services were not in demand.

Shortly before the war in Europe finished the *Albatross* was placed in the Reserve Fleet for about a year. Then, unlike so many of our ageing and surplus warships, she was not to suffer the common fate of going to the breaker's yard. In 1946 she was sold and became the merchant ship *Hellenic Prince*, in which unusual guise she continued to give useful service for many years.

LEADING PARTICULARS

Displacement: 4,800 tons.

Dimensions: Length, 443 ft. Beam, 61 ft.

Machinery: Geared Turbines, 12,000 S.H.P. Speed: 21 knots.

Armament: Four 4·7 in. A.A. Plus several 20 mm. on conversion to repair ship.

Aircraft: 9.

Complement: 450.

Ark Royal 1937

FOR more than a decade after the *Glorious* had been converted, the Navy struggled on with its six existing carriers. These were the lean years for the three services and naval aviation was fairly well down on the list of defence priorities. Then came the first glint in this gloomy picture—the *Ark Royal*.

Launched in 1937, she was completed towards the end of 1938; embodied in her was all the past experience of carrier construction and operating. Approximately 800 ft. of clear flight deck, apart from the small 'island' on the starboard side, was available for her aircraft. She could accommodate 60 aircraft in her two hangars, which ran almost the length of the ship; in addition she had three aircraft lifts, two catapults, an emergency crash barrier, and arrester wires that were raised and lowered hydraulically.

Compared with the earlier carriers her accommodation was exceptionally comfortable; a great step forward had been made with the internal arrangements for aircraft maintenance, stowage and supplies of stores. With a strong anti-aircraft armament, much more suitably sited than in the earlier ships, and a high turn of speed, this was an aircraft carrier that the Navy could be proud of. All the large fleet carriers to follow were strongly influenced by her design.

A few months before the war started the *Ark*, as she was affectionately called by all who served in her, escorted the King and Queen some of the way down the English Channel on their official visit to Canada. As soon as the Royal couple were out of sight flying training re-commenced. The ship was equipped with Blackburn Skuas, fighter/dive-bombers, and Fairey Swordfish, reconnaissance and torpedo bomber. Intensive day and night flying exercises were carried out by both types of aircraft; when the war started the carrier was fully operational and ready.

The first enemy aircraft in the Second World War to be destroyed by the British was shot down by one of the *Ark*'s Skuas. This occurred on the 26th September, 1939, when the carrier, with the Home Fleet, was escorting a damaged submarine across the North Sea. (The crew of the Skua were Lieutenant B. S. McEwen and Petty Officer Airman B. M. Seymour). About this time the Germans claimed that they had sunk the *Ark*; the attack had in fact been a very near miss with a 2,000 lb. bomb. Shortly after this incident the carrier went to the South Atlantic to join in the hunt for the *Graf Spee*. Although her aircraft searched several million square miles they did not spot the pocket battleship which, after the action with three British cruisers off the River Plate, scuttled herself. Returning to the U.K. shortly after this long search, she was engaged on anti-submarine patrols.

In company with the *Glorious* the *Ark* arrived off the Norwegian coast on the 24th April, 1940; she carried two Skua and two Swordfish squadrons and was the flagship of the carrier force. The carriers bore the brunt of the air defence, as mentioned earlier in the chapter on the *Glorious*. Suffice to say that her work in Norway was valuable; her aircraft carried out numerous sorties, in bad weather, against a far superior enemy.

Shortly after the ill-fated Norwegian campaign ended, the main theatre of naval operations shifted to the Mediterranean and North Africa; Italy had entered the war and France had collapsed. The *Ark* was present at Oran in the sad action carried out to ensure that the French Fleet would not be a menace. In July 1940 her Swordfish aircraft carried out several damaging attacks on the Sardinian airfield of Elmas. After this the carrier joined, and became an integral part of, Force H.

Note:—Force H was the name given to a compact striking force of warships based on Gibraltar; their broad terms of reference were operations in the Western Mediterranean but

Ark Royal, perhaps the most famous carrier ever.

they were also available for work in the Atlantic when needed. Apart from the *Ark*, the other permanent ships in this force were the battle cruiser *Renown* and the cruiser *Sheffield;* from time to time they were joined by other major warships as required.

With Force H the *Ark* escorted many convoys to Malta; her fighters were so efficient that they accounted for more than 100 enemy aircraft during her career. In February 1941 came a major action with the bombardment of Genoa.

Enemy spies were deliberately allowed to learn (this was not hard with the fleet based at Gibraltar) that an important operation was pending and that major warships would be going to Malta or even further eastwards. The fleet left Gibraltar and headed eastwards but, in the middle of the Western Mediterranean, turned north for Genoa, off where they arrived near dawn on the 9th February. Thanks to the security 'leak' the enemy had concentrated their aircraft in Southern Italy. Aircraft from the *Ark* spotted for the battleships' guns which caused tremendous damage ashore. Whilst the bom-

bardment was going on other aircraft from the carrier made a diversionary raid on Pisa. This brilliantly planned and executed operation thoroughly confused and upset the Italians; the fleet suffered no casualties and returned to Gibraltar safely.

On the 26th May, 1941, the German battleship *Bismarck* had eluded her pursuers in the Atlantic and was making for Brest; Force H had been called into the gigantic operation and was steaming towards the area. Fortunately, a Swordfish from the *Ark* spotted her and stayed shadowing. In terrible weather the carrier launched a striking force of 15 Swordfish, led by Lieutenant Commander T. P. Coode, which scored three torpedo hits. The battleship's steering gear was seriously damaged and her speed reduced; a few hours later the rest of the fleet caught up and destroyed her.

After this episode the *Ark* returned to the Mediterranean and continued to give her protection to the Malta Convoys. She seemed to bear a charmed life, for more often than not she was the primary target for the enemy and had

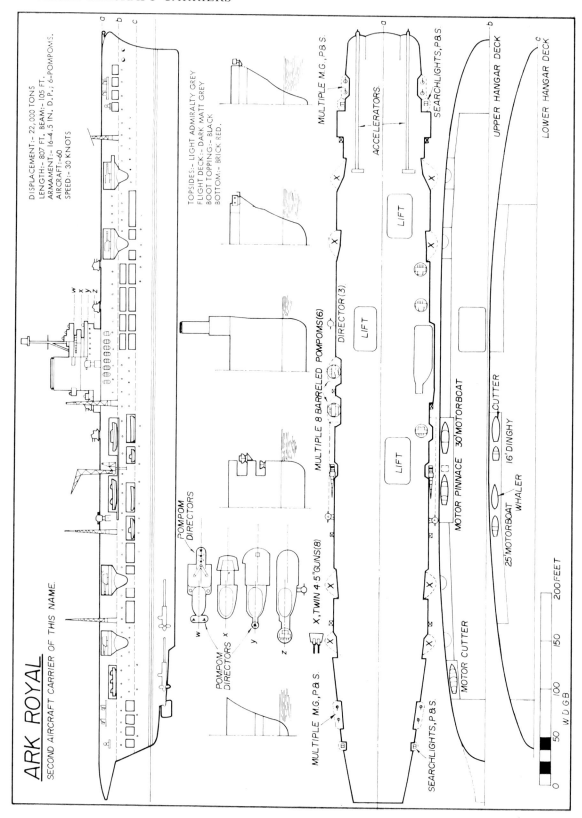

ARK ROYAL
SECOND AIRCRAFT CARRIER OF THIS NAME.

DISPLACEMENT:- 22,000 TONS
LENGTH:- 807 FT. BEAM:- 105 FT.
ARMAMENT:- 16-4.5 IN., D.P.; 6-POMPOMS.
AIRCRAFT:-60
SPEED:- 30 KNOTS

TOPSIDES:- LIGHT ADMIRALTY GREY
FLIGHT DECK:- DARK MATT GREY
BOOT TOPPING:- BLACK
BOTTOM:- BRICK RED.

POMPOM DIRECTORS

POMPOM DIRECTORS x

w

y

z

X, TWIN 4.5" GUNS (8)

MULTIPLE M.G., P & S.

MULTIPLE 8 BARRELED POMPOMS (6)

MULTIPLE M.G., P & S.

SEARCHLIGHTS, P & S.

DIRECTOR (3)

ACCELERATORS.

LIFT

LIFT

LIFT

SEARCHLIGHTS, P & S.

MOTOR CUTTER

25' MOTORBOAT
WHALER

MOTOR PINNACE 30' MOTORBOAT

16' DINGHY

CUTTER

UPPER HANGAR DECK

LOWER HANGAR DECK

W D G B

0   50   100   150   200 FEET

several near misses. Then, on the 13th November, 1941, she was torpedoed by a German submarine. Her gallant crew did their best to get their ship back to Gibraltar, but unfortunately, almost within sight of the base, she finally sank. With the sole, and sad, exception of one seaman, the rest of her crew survived.

LEADING PARTICULARS

Displacement: 22,000 tons.

Dimensions: Length, 807 ft. Beam, 105 ft.

Machinery: Geared Turbines. Speed: 30 knots.

Armament: 16 4·5 in. D.P.; six multiple pom poms.

Aircraft: 60.   Complement: 1,575.

Ark Royal

H.M.S. Implacable

Illustrious
Group   1940

THE six ships of this group, in their order of completion, were:—*Illustrious* (May 1940), *Formidable* (November 1940), *Victorious* (May 1941), *Indomitable* (August 1941), *Indefatigable* (May 1944), and *Implacable* (August 1944).

I think it is more accurate to refer to these ships as a group because, although generally similar in appearance, there were enough differences to justify this terminology. The last two ships were slightly larger and incorporated several modifications; the *Victorious*, still in service, bears little resemblance to the original design and will be dealt with later as a separate subject. Meanwhile, the other five ships deserve individual mention, especially the *Illustrious*, and their histories follow.

ILLUSTRIOUS

With her armoured flight deck and radar, the *Illustrious* was a very welcome addition to the Mediterranean Fleet which she joined, shortly after her completion, in August 1940. Her operational career began on the 4th September when her aircraft bombed Kalatho in Rhodes. On the 16th September shipping was attacked in Benghazi and two Italian destroyers—the *Borea* and *Aquilone*—were sunk. Still in September, the 29th, she left Alexandria with the Fleet to cover reinforcements for Malta.

October, 1940, was another busy month starting with another Malta convoy on the 11th/12th. On the 14th her aircraft made a moonlight attack on Porto Lago, Leros, achieving complete surprise and dropping 92 bombs which caused considerable damage. Tobruk was the next target, on the night of the 23rd/24th, when her aircraft laid mines off the harbour and also carried out a high level raid.

The most spectacular achievement of her career was the attack on Taranto on the night of the 11th/12th November, which resulted in half the Italian battle fleet being put out of action; through this action the balance of naval power was altered, in favour of the hard pressed British, overnight. On the 26th, Porto Lago, Leros, was again bombed, which resulted in fires being started in the dockyard and a ship was left burning. In addition to the work of her Swordfish aircraft, her fighters had shot down 21 enemy aircraft in this intensive period of 12 weeks' operations.

In December she operated off the Libyan coast, in co-operation with the advance of General Wavell's Army, and also assisted in operations off Greece. On the 21st, nine of her aircraft attacked an enemy convoy off Kerkenah island and destroyed two ships; during the same night Tripoli was raided by her aircraft.

The Axis powers were furious that this ship was sailing around the Mediterranean creating a trail of havoc and destruction, so, in January 1941, German aircraft arrived in Sicily to destroy her. On the 10th January, during the passage of an important convoy to Malta, the Germans made the *Illustrious* their main target; a direct hit was scored, resulting in serious damage and heavy casualties. Through the determined efforts of her crew she managed to reach Malta where, on the 16th and 19th, she was again hit during air raids. On the night of the 23rd she was got away and reached Alexandria on the 25th. After temporary repairs there she left for the U.S.A. on the 10th March, via the Cape of Good Hope, and remained there until December undergoing repairs.

As soon as her repairs were completed the *Illustrious* was allocated to the Eastern Fleet under Admiral Sir James Somerville. In May 1942 she took part in the landing operations in Madagascar which resulted in the capture of the naval base at Diego Saurez. Later that year, in the September, she was present in the further operations off Madagascar which resulted in the complete occupation of the island.

In January 1943 she was withdrawn from the

Illustrious

Eastern Fleet for improvements in her fighter direction and radar equipment; a refit was also carried out at Liverpool. Joining the Home Fleet in July she took part, during that month, in an operation off Southern Norway which was designed to pin down enemy forces whilst the Allies invaded Sicily. On the 13th August she left for her old hunting grounds, the Mediterranean; she was present at the Salerno landings on the 9th September. After a refit in the Clyde, during November, she was again allocated to the Eastern Fleet and arrived at Colombo on the 30th January, 1944.

During the next 12 months she took part in several operations by the Eastern Fleet which included the following:—

February—movement to intercept a possible blockade runner from Japan to Germany in the Indian Ocean.

19th April—air strike on Sabang.

17th May—air strike on Surabaya.

21st June—air strike on Port Blair, Andaman Islands.

25th July—air strike and bombardment on Sabang.

20th December—air strike on Belawan Deli, Sumatra.

24th January, 1945—air strike on Palembang, Southern Sumatra.

In February 1945 the *Illustrious* was transferred to the newly formed British Pacific Fleet. During March and April she took part in the Allied offensive towards the Japanese mainland —Operation 'Iceberg'. Her aircraft made attacks on airfields in the Sakishima group of islands to prevent the Japanese using them for staging aircraft. Being in need of further repairs, she was relieved in the Pacific by the *Formidable*. She left Fremantle on the 29th May for the U.K., and arrived at Rosyth on the 27th June where she was refitted.

Early in 1947 she became the trials carrier and as such, with new aircraft entering service, was kept very busy. The then First Lord of the Admiralty, Lord Pakenham, on the 23rd July, 1951, made history by landing on her deck in the English Channel—the first holder of his office to do so. After many years of valiant service the *Illustrious* was scrapped.

FORMIDABLE

In the early part of 1941, shortly after her completion in the previous November, the *Formidable* joined the Mediterranean Fleet; with her sister ship, *Illustrious*, completely out of action, she was an extremely welcome ship to the hard-pressed fleet.

On the 28th March, 1941, an R.A.F. reconnaissance aircraft reported a force of Italian warships 100 miles East of Sicily steering eastwards; their target was, almost certainly, the British convoys that were on their way to Greece. The fleet left Alexandria to counter this threat and at six o'clock the next morning the *Formidable* flew off four Albacores and one Swordfish to search the area between Crete and Cyrenaica; the Italian force was spotted just over an hour later.

The carrier had available 10 Albacores, four Swordfish and 13 Fulmars, and at 10 a.m. six Albacores and two escorting Fulmars were flown off to intercept the enemy. Just as the torpedo aircraft were going into the attack they were intercepted by two German Ju.88s, but one of these was immediately shot down by the fighters and the other made off; one certain torpedo hit was observed on the Italian battleship *Vittorio Veneto* which lost speed and her steering appeared to be out of action.

Throughout the day the carrier launched several attacks against the Italian force, which had been joined by three more large cruisers and additional destroyers, through extremely heavy anti-aircraft fire. Towards sunset one of her aircraft got a hit on the cruiser *Pola* which stopped her. During the night action that followed, off Cape Matapan, this ship and her sister ships— *Zara* and *Fiume*—were sunk by gunfire, along with two destroyers, by the British battleships. The next morning further searches failed to find the Italian battleship but the carrier's aircraft carried out more humane work in directing ships to the enemy survivors. As a direct result of this action, which without the *Formidable* would not have been possible, Admiral Cunningham was able to transport and later evacuate our troops from Greece and Crete. From a strict naval aviation point of view this action was not completely satisfying in that the carrier did not have enough aircraft, at that time, to maintain continuous touch with the separate Italian force and, at the same time, build up the strike force necessary to sink or stop a modern capital ship.

From the 24th April, 1941, to the 2nd May, the *Formidable* provided air cover during the evacuation from Greece. During the evacuation from Crete she was the only carrier available, and operated with the Mediterranean Fleet. On the 26th May, just after her Albacores and Fulmars had returned from a successful raid on Scarpanto airfield in the Dodecanese, she was hit twice by enemy bombers. She was able to make Alexandria under her own steam but could take no further part in these operations.

After her long period of repairs and refit she came back to the Mediterranean to take part in the Salerno landings and other operations in the period from September 1943 to September 1944. From there she went on to the Far East and took part in several operations including the first Anglo-American attack on the Japanese mainland in July 1945. In the May of that year she was hit by a Japanese suicide aircraft but, thanks mainly to her armoured flight deck, was soon back in action again.

From the end of the war until 1947 she was employed on trooping duties which included bringing home from the East many prisoners of war. On her return she was placed in the reserve and not used again in an active capacity. In 1953 she was sold for breaking up.

INDOMITABLE

The *Indomitable* was first commissioned on the 26th August, 1941, and in October proceeded to the America and West Indies Station. In December she was ordered to the Middle East to embark aircraft for Batavia and arrived at Port Sudan on the 14th January, 1942. She left the next day with the aircraft and all were safely flown off on the 27th and 28th January. More

Indomitable

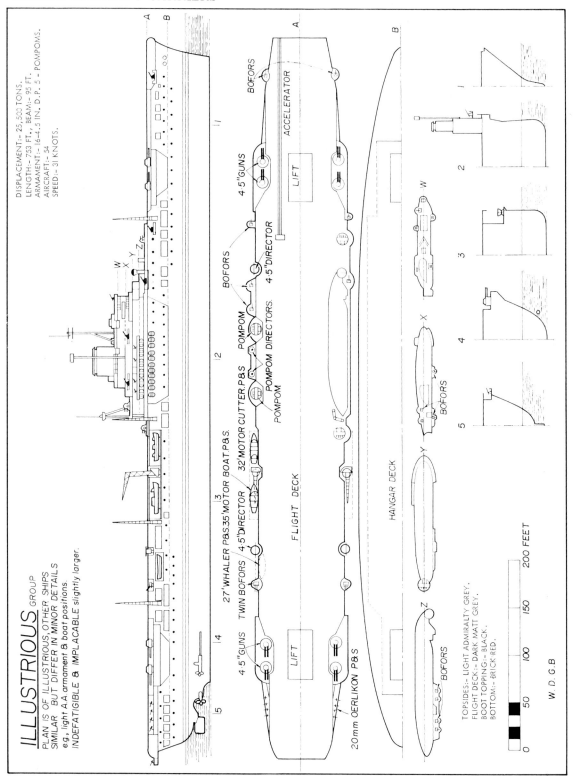

ILLUSTRIOUS GROUP

PLAN IS OF ILLUSTRIOUS, OTHER SHIPS SIMILAR BUT DIFFER IN MINOR DETAILS e.g., light A.A. armament & boat positions. INDEFATIGIBLE & IMPLACABLE slightly larger.

DISPLACEMENT:- 25,500 TONS.
LENGTH:- 753 FT., BEAM:- 95 FT.
ARMAMENT:- 16-4.5 IN. D.P. 5 - POMPOMS.
AIRCRAFT:- 54
SPEED:- 31 KNOTS.

BOFORS

4.5"GUNS

ACCELERATOR

LIFT

BOFORS

4.5"DIRECTOR

POMPOM

POMPOM DIRECTORS.

POMPOM

FLIGHT DECK

HANGAR DECK

27' WHALER P&S 35'MOTOR BOAT P&S.
4.5"DIRECTOR 32'MOTOR CUTTER.P&S.
TWIN BOFORS

4.5"GUNS

LIFT

20mm OERLIKON P&S

BOFORS

W

X

Y

Z

BOFORS

TOPSIDES:- LIGHT ADMIRALTY GREY.
FLIGHT DECK:- DARK MATT GREY.
BOOT TOPPING:- BLACK.
BOTTOM:- BRICK RED.

0   50   100   150   200 FEET

W. D. G. B

66

E*

aircraft ferrying operations to the Far East were carried out during February and March and then she joined the Eastern Fleet in her proper guise as an aircraft carrier.

In May the *Indomitable* provided air cover in the operations to capture the naval and air base at Diego Saurez in Madagascar. The following month she took part in searches for Japanese commerce raiders and after this left for the Mediterranean. Taking part in Operation Pedestal on the 12th August, a large convoy for the relief of Malta, she was hit by three bombs and had several near misses. Badly damaged, she returned to Gibraltar at reduced speed and then proceeded to Liverpool for more permanent repairs.

Seven months later, March 1943, she joined the Home Fleet for a short time. Once again she returned to the Mediterranean, in the June of that year, to take part in the covering and supporting forces for the invasion of Sicily. On the 16th July she was torpedoed abreast the port boiler room, during an attack by enemy aircraft, but was able to proceed to Malta under her own power. Once again she had to retire for permanent repairs, and this time she went to the U.S.A., arriving at Norfolk, Virginia, on the 1st September.

When these repairs were completed in March 1944, the *Indomitable* left for the U.K. and arrived at Rosyth on the 2nd May. On the 12th June she left the Clyde to join the Eastern Fleet and arrived at Trincomalee on the 25th July. From then until the end of the year she was actively engaged in air strike operations on objectives in Sumatra and the Nicobar Islands.

During January 1945, she was engaged in further air strikes on Japanese oil installations in Sumatra; in February she proceeded to Fremantle to join the newly formed British Pacific Fleet. In March, as part of the American operations against Okinawa, the British Pacific Fleet—after working up at Manus—sailed from the Carolines to neutralise the enemy airfields in the Sakishama group. On the 26th and 27th March aircraft from the *Indomitable* made a series of attacks on enemy airfields; six more attacks were carried out during the following 31 days the Fleet was at sea. On the 13th April she was near-missed by a bomb which fortunately failed to explode.

The Fleet left Leyte for further air strikes on the 1st May and on the 4th the *Indomitable* and *Formidable* were both damaged by Japanese suicide attacks. One bomb bounced off the *Indomitable* and another missed by only 10 yds.; fortunately the carrier received only superficial

Implacable

damage. The Fleet returned to Manus on the 30th May and, from there, she sailed for Australian waters.

Leaving Sydney on the 15th August, the *Indomitable* joined a Task Group for the relief of Hong Kong, returning from there to Sydney on the 22nd October for a brief call before returning to the U.K. on the 30th November. She continued to serve, with the Home and Mediterranean Fleets, for a few years giving useful service. In 1955, after more lucky escapes from catastrophe than most ships, she went to the breaker's yard.

INDEFATIGABLE
and
IMPLACABLE

These two ships were slightly larger, a little faster and differed in the design of the bows and stern compared with the earlier ships of this group; generally speaking they had a much heavier looking appearance. The only difference between these two otherwise identical sister ships was that the boats on the *Indefatigable* were stowed one deck higher. Although ordered just before the war, they were not completed until 1944, in May and August respectively.

Both ships spent most of their war service in the Far East operating with the British Pacific Fleet. Before going to the Far East aircraft from the *Implacable* located the German battleship *Tirpitz* in a new berth at Tromso, Norway; four weeks later she was sunk by R.A.F. heavy bombers. In the Far East both ships took part in many air strikes against the Japanese held islands and, during one of these, the *Indefatigable* was hit by a suicide aircraft but suffered only slight damage.

After the Japanese surrender, the *Implacable* was employed as a prisoner of war evacuation ship between Manilla, Hong Kong and the Canadian ports of Esquimalt and Vancouver before returning to the U.K.; the *Indefatigable* had returned home earlier and been placed in the Reserve Fleet.

During 1948 to 1949 the *Implacable* was refitted and became flagship of the Home Fleet from May 1949 until July 1950; after this she was refitted for service in the Training Squadron from November 1951. In the summer of 1954 she went back into the reserve and was scrapped the following year. The *Indefatigable* remained in the reserve after the war until 1949; in 1950 she was refitted for the Training Squadron. Like her sister ship she returned to the reserve in the summer of 1954 and was scrapped in 1955.

LEADING PARTICULARS

Illustrious, Formidable and *Indomitable*
Displacement: 25,500 tons.
Length: 753 ft. Beam: 95 ft. (not including Sponsons).
Machinery: Geared Turbines, 110,000 S.H.P. Speed, 31 knots.
Armament: 16 4·5 in. D.P. 2pdr. multiple pom poms, plus 40 and 20 mm. A.A.
Aircraft: 54. (*Indomitable* had extra hangar space and could carry 65).

Complement: 1,600.

Indefatigable and *Implacable*
Displacement: 26,000 tons.
Length: 766 ft. Beam: 95¾ ft. (extreme width, 131¼ ft.).
Machinery: Geared Turbines, 148,000 S.H.P. Speed, 32½ knots.
Armament: As for *Illustrious* but carried a larger number of smaller guns.
Aircraft: 72.
Complement: 1,785 (peace); 2,200 (wartime).

Unicorn 1943

HAD the Second World War not intervened, the *Unicorn* would most likely have been omitted from this book. Originally ordered under the 1938 Estimates as an aircraft supply and maintenance ship, it was envisaged, at that time, that she would undertake duties in much the same way as a submarine depot ship acts for submarines. As such she would probably not have had a flight deck nor would she have emerged as an aircraft carrier in appearance. With two hangars, one above the other, she had an extremely top heavy look—on such a comparatively short length—which gave her a unique shape amongst our carriers.

Soon after she had been laid down, June 1939, it was decided to continue her future construction on the lines of an aircraft carrier and she was completed as such in March 1943. Her first operation was at Salerno in the same year where her aircraft—Seafires—gave support and fighter cover to the landings. After this she carried out various convoy escort duties and eventually joined the British Pacific Fleet. There she took part in several operations, of which the most notable was the attack on Okinawa.

In January 1946 the *Unicorn* returned home from the Far East to Devonport; the next three years were spent in reserve. Required for service again in the Far East, she was brought out of the reserve and prepared for duty. On the 18th September, 1949, she left the Clyde, with a load of transit aircraft and arrived in Singapore on the 21st October.

It had been intended that she should return by September 1950, but in June that year the War in Korea broke out, and she remained in the Far East throughout that conflict; she eventually arrived back at Devonport again on the 17th September, 1953. Her main duties in the Korean War were to keep the more operational carriers of the British Fleet supplied with aircraft and essential aircraft engines and spare parts.

In addition to her normal work, the *Unicorn* was much in demand as a troopship. In August 1950 she carried the 1st Battalion, The Middlesex Regiment from Hong Kong to Pusan—these were the first British troops to land in Korea. Altogether she carried several thousands of passengers, of all three services, to and from the fighting.

When she returned to the U.K. she was placed once more in the reserve, where the rest of her service was spent, until it was decided to scrap her in 1958.

LEADING PARTICULARS

Displacement: 14,750 tons.
Length: 640 ft. Beam: 90 ft.
Machinery: Geared Turbines; 40,000 S.H.P.; Speed, 24 knots.
Armament: 8-4 in. A.A.; 16 2pdr. pom poms.
Aircraft: 35 could be carried when she was an operational carrier.
Complement: About 1,100.

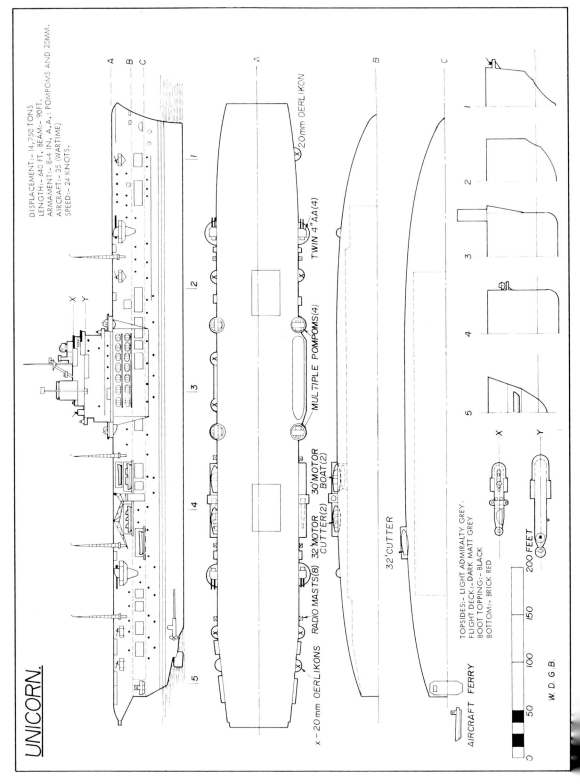

UNICORN.

DISPLACEMENT:- 14,750 TONS
LENGTH:- 640 FT. BEAM:- 90FT.
ARMAMENT:- 8·4 IN, A.A.:- POMPOMS AND 20MM.
AIRCRAFT:- 35 (WARTIME)
SPEED:- 24 KNOTS.

x – 20mm OERLIKONS

RADIO MASTS(8)

32'MOTOR CUTTER(2)

30'MOTOR BOAT(2)

MULTIPLE POMPOMS(4)

TWIN 4"AA(4)

x 20mm OERLIKON

32'CUTTER

AIRCRAFT FERRY

TOPSIDES:- LIGHT ADMIRALTY GREY.
FLIGHT DECK:- DARK MATT GREY
BOOT TOPPING:- BLACK
BOTTOM:- BRICK RED

0   50   100   150   200 FEET

W. D. G. B.

(Imperial War Museum photo)

Two pictures of H.M.S. Unicorn

H.M.S. Campania

Escort Carriers 1941

IN all 45 Escort carriers served with the Royal Navy during the Second World War; of these six were built by the British and no less than 39 by the U.S.A. Their service took them all over the world and they operated in most of the war theatres, including the following: Atlantic and Arctic convoys, the Salerno landings, operations off the Norwegian coast, the invasion of Southern France and many operations in the Pacific. Comparatively speaking, their losses were light, in view of the large number of them, only three being sunk—*Audacity*, *Avenger* and *Dasher*.

Basically all these carriers were merchant ships, either already built or building, up to the main deck; existing or intended superstructure was eliminated and a flight deck and hangar space took their place. They were manned by naval crews, as opposed to merchant service personnel in the Merchant aircraft carrier—more about these later—and their role was purely flying operations. There was one major difference between the British and American built carriers, in that the latter had a wooden planked flight deck as opposed to steel plating in the British.

British Built

Audacity

This was the first ever escort carrier and had been a German ship (*Hannover*) captured early in the war; her career was short but successful—described in 1939 to 1945 period. Displacement: 5,537 tons. Length: 475 ft. Beam: 56 ft. Aircraft: Six (Martlets).

Activity

Similar to above ship but slightly larger.

Pretoria Castle

An ex-liner which was the largest of the Escort carriers. She gave good service as a training carrier and was converted back to her former role after the war. Displacement: 17,392 tons. Length: 594 ft. Beam: 76 ft. Aircraft: 20 plus.

Campania, *Nairana* and *Vindex*

Slightly larger than the American built ships, these three were named after seaplane carriers of the First World War. While the other two were converted back to mercantile roles shortly after the war, the *Campania* remained in service for a few years and, in the early fifties, became a floating fair ship for British industry. Displacement: 12,450 tons. Length: 540 ft. Beam: 70 ft. Aircraft: 20.

American Built

These fell into two classes, the *Archer* and *Ruler*. The first class was slightly smaller and not all of them had their hangar protected from the sea for its full length; the *Archer* and other earlier ships in this class had protection built in to the rear third of the hangar sides. When the war ended all these ships were returned to the U.S.A. under the Lease Lend agreement.

Archer Class (25 Ships)

Arbiter, Archer, Attacker, Battler, Biter, Chaser, Fencer, Hunter, Patroller, Puncher, Pursuer, Ravager, Reaper, Searcher, Slinger, Smiter, Speaker, Stalker, Striker, Tracker, Trouncer, Trumpeter. The *Avenger* and *Dasher* were lost.

Displacement: 10,000 to 12,000 tons. Length: 492-6 ft. Beam: 70 ft.

Ruler Class (14 Ships)

Ameer, Atheling, Begum, Emperor, Empress, Khedive, Nabob, Premier, Queen, Rajah, Ranee, Ruler, Shah, Thane.

This class had a larger displacement and were slightly longer and wider (514 ft. × 80 ft.).

MERCHANT AIRCRAFT CARRIERS

These ships, all British built, were much less sophisticated than the Escort carrier. All sailed under the Red Ensign and were manned by merchant service crews—only their air and ground crew were naval personnel. They were adapted from grain carriers and oil tankers,

H.M.S. Nairana

H.M.S. Khedive

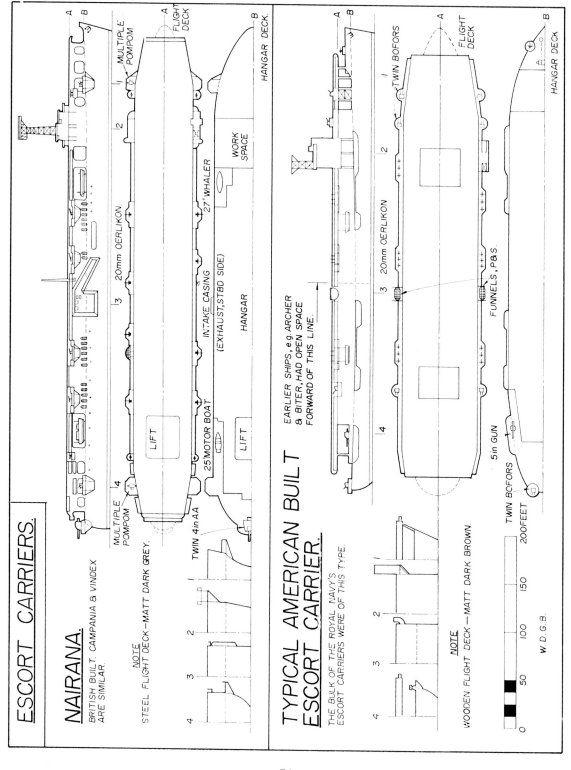

ESCORT CARRIERS.

NAIRANA.

BRITISH BUILT. CAMPANIA & VINDEX
ARE SIMILAR.

NOTE
STEEL FLIGHT DECK—MATT DARK GREY.

MULTIPLE POM-POM

20mm OERLIKON

FLIGHT DECK

HANGAR DECK.

WORK SPACE

27' WHALER

INTAKE CASING
(EXHAUST, STBD SIDE)

HANGAR

LIFT

25' MOTOR BOAT

LIFT

MULTIPLE POMPOM

TWIN 4in AA

TYPICAL AMERICAN BUILT
ESCORT CARRIER.

THE BULK OF THE ROYAL NAVY'S
ESCORT CARRIERS WERE OF THIS TYPE.

NOTE
WOODEN FLIGHT DECK—MATT DARK BROWN.

EARLIER SHIPS, e.g. ARCHER
& BITER, HAD OPEN SPACE
FORWARD OF THIS LINE.

TWIN BOFORS

FLIGHT DECK

HANGAR DECK

20mm OERLIKON

FUNNELS, P&S.

5in GUN

TWIN BOFORS

W.D.G.B.

0   50   100   150   200 FEET

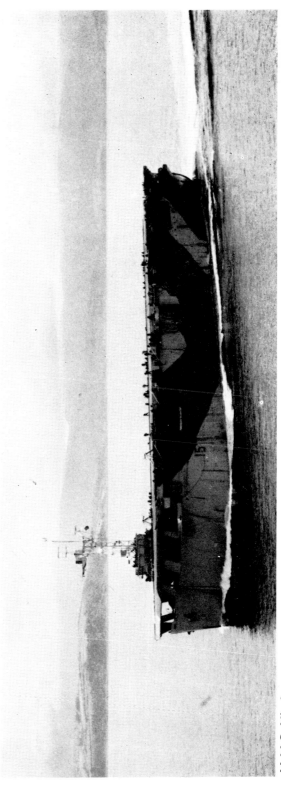

H.M.S. Vindex

which had no hatches and derricks like other cargo ships, and were used in the dual role of merchant ship and escort carrier during their service.

The oil tankers had a longer flight deck and the aircraft were stowed permanently in the open; the shorter grain carriers had a small hangar and lift for their aircraft. Superseding the earlier CAM ships (Catapult Armed Merchantman) these merchant carriers carried four aircraft—usually Swordfish.

Ex Grain Carriers

All had the prefix Empire: *Macalpine,* *Mackendrick, Macandrew, Macdermott, Macrae* and *Maccallum.*

Displacement: 8,000 tons (gross); all reverted to mercantile use after the war.

Ex Tankers

These four ships were various tankers, around 9,000 tons, all reverted to mercantile use after the war; all had the prefix Empire: *Mackay, Maccol, Macmahon* and *Maccabe.*

The following were all tankers of the *Rapana* class, about 8,000 tons, which reverted to mercantile use after the war:

Acavus, Adula, Alexia, Amastra, Ancylus, Gadila, Macorna, Miralda and *Rapana.*

H.M.S. Theseus

Light Fleet Carriers 1944

Strictly speaking there were two classes of these ships which consist of:—

Glory Class—10 Ships

Glory, Ocean, Theseus, Triumph, Vengeance, Warrior, Colossus, Venerable, Perseus and Pioneer.

Majestic Class—6 Ships

Hercules, Leviathan, Powerful, Magnificent, Majestic and Terrible.

Laid down in late 1942 and early 1943, these ships were designed to many of the specifications required for merchant ships. It was intended, after the war, that they could be converted for mercantile use; none, however, were converted as their subsequent histories will show. None of the Majestic class ever served with the Royal Navy.

Externally there was little difference between the two classes and they had the same dimensions and machinery. One slight external difference, though, was the armament—in the Majestic class it originally consisted of 30-40 mm. (6 twin and 18 single mountings); in the Glory class it was mixed 40 mm. and 2pdr. pom poms as shown in the leading particulars.

Internally the Majestic class had much better accommodation for the ratings, in that they were provided with separate dining rooms and living quarters. Such was not the case in the Glory class, where the ratings ate, lived and slept in the same crowded space.

Although smaller and slower than the Fleet Carriers, they were certainly more economical to operate and presented a vast improvement over the earlier Escort Carriers. For many post-war years the Glory class bore the brunt of naval aviation, especially during the Korean War, until the gradual advent of heavier and faster jet aircraft. Only the Triumph remains in the Royal Navy now, as an Escort Maintenance Ship with additional superstructure, but several continue to give service in other navies. A very brief outline of each ship follows:—

Glory

Completed 2.4.45. Served in Korean War. Scrapped in 1961.

Ocean

Completed 30.6.45. Served in Korean War. Scrapped in 1962.

Theseus

Completed 9.1.46. Fitted with one four-bladed and one three-bladed propellor to minimise vibration. Served in Korean War. Scrapped in 1962.

Triumph

Completed 9.4.46. Served in Korean War. Converted to Escort Maintenance Ship 1958 to 1965. Still in service.

Vengeance

Completed 15.1.45. Carried out experimental Arctic cruise 1949. Lent to Australian Navy 1953 to 1955. Modernised 1956 to 1961 and sold to Brazil 1961. Re-named Minas Gerais.

Warrior

Completed 24.1.46. Experimentally fitted with flexible flight deck 1948 for aircraft landing with skids; this was not successful and flexible deck was removed. Acted as aircraft transport and troopship during period of Korean War. Sold to Argentina in 1958. Re-named Independencia.

Colossus

Completed 16.12.44. Lent to France in 1946 with the option of purchase in 1951. The option was taken up and she was permanently transferred to France that year. Re-named Arromanches.

Venerable

Completed 17.1.45. Purchased by Holland in 1948 and has been considerably modernised. Re-named Karel Doorman.

Perseus and Pioneer

Both completed in 1945, with no armament, as aircraft maintenance carriers. Scrapped in 1958 and 1954 respectively.

H.M.S. Venerable

H.M.S. Vengeance

H.M.S. Glory

H.M.S. Theseus

When the war ended most of the *Majestic* class were in an advanced stage of completion but, with changing requirements in naval aviation and without the impetus of wartime construction, they lay around for many years before final completion as shown below.

Hercules
Laid down 14.10.43. Completed in 1961 and purchased by India. Re-named *Vikrant*.

Leviathan
Laid down 18.10.43. After 75 per cent of construction had been carried out work was stopped and she is still laid up in this state. No decision has been announced about her future.

Powerful
Laid down 27.11.43. Completed for Canada in 1957. Re-named *Bonaventure*.

Magnificent
Completed in 1948. Then lent and sold to Canada. Scrapped in 1958.

Majestic
Laid down 15.4.43. Completed for Australia in 1955. Re-named *Melbourne*.

Terrible
Completed in 1949 for Australia. Served in Korean War. Converted into fast military transport in 1962. Re-named *Sydney*.

LEADING PARTICULARS
Displacement: 13,300 tons (average standard, very minor differences).
Length: 695 ft. Beam: 80 ft. (maximum width, $112\frac{1}{2}$ ft.).
Machinery: Geared Turbines, 40,000 S.H.P. Speed: 25 knots.
Armament: 19 40 mm.; 24 2pdr. pom poms (six quadruple mountings).
Aircraft: Officially 39 to 44 (during Korean War *Theseus* carried 23 Sea Furies and 12 Fireflies, plus one Sea Otter and one U.S. Helicopter).
Complement: Around 1,100.

F*

Eagle

1951

ORIGINALLY ordered on the 19th May, 1942, the construction of this ship took almost ten years. Delays were inevitable with the end of the war and, also, with the advent of the heavier jet aircraft to naval aviation. Laid down on the 24th October, 1942, she was launched on the 19th March, 1946. Finally completed on the 1st October, 1951, the *Eagle* was accepted into the service in March 1952. Displacing just over 54,000 tons, at full load, she is the largest ship ever to serve in the Royal Navy.

Until 1959 there was no angled flight deck and her armament consisted of 16, 4·5-in. dual purpose guns mounted in eight twin turrets; in addition she carried over fifty 40 mm. Bofors guns in single, twin and quadruple mountings. However, when her reconstruction was carried out, eight 4·5-in. guns were removed from the forward part of the ship; all the 40 mm. were removed and in their place has been substituted six 'Seacat' Surface to Air Missile Launchers (S.A.M.). The photographs show clearly the major differences before and after reconstruction.

The reconstruction and modernisation process took four and a half years—from the end of 1959 until the 14th May, 1962. Included in this work were the fitting of more efficient steam catapults, a fully angled flight deck of $8\frac{1}{2}$ degrees, 948 'Searchlight' radar, a slightly larger 'island' and improved living accommodation. Before leaving the subject of building and reconstruction, it is interesting to note the costs involved in these processes; initial building cost was £15,795,000 and subsequent reconstruction cost nearly twice as much—£31,000,000.

Aircraft carried, at the present time, are the Sea Vixen (Night All-Weather Fighter), Buccaneer (Strike Aircraft), Scimitar (Ground Attack plus In-Flight Refuelling Tanker), Gannet (Airborne Early Warning Aircraft) and

H.M.S. Eagle

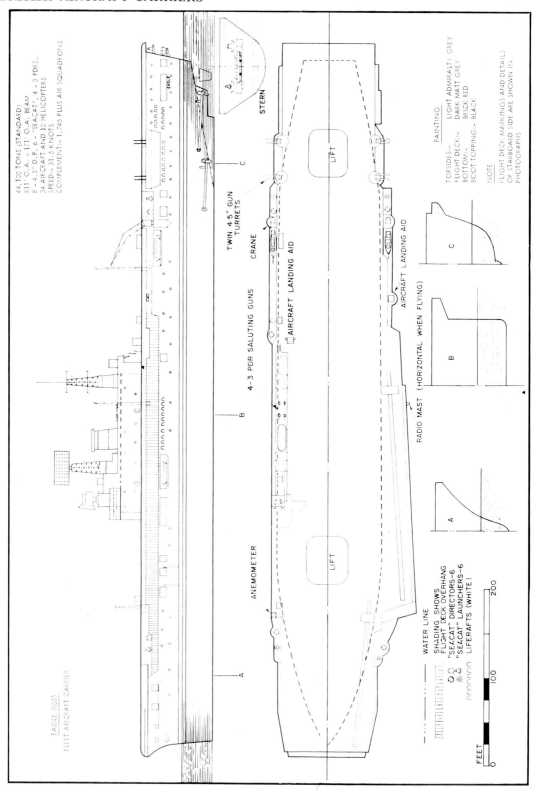

EAGLE (R05)
FLEET AIRCRAFT CARRIER

44,100 TONS (STANDARD)
811' O.A. x 171' O.A. BEAM
8 – 4.5" D.P. 6 – "SEACAT", 4 – 3 PDRS.
34 AIRCRAFT AND 10 HELICOPTERS
SPEED – 31.5 KNOTS
COMPLEMENT – 1,745 PLUS AIR SQUADRONS

PAINTING

TOPSIDES:- LIGHT ADMIRALTY GREY
FLIGHT DECK:- DARK MATT GREY
BOTTOM:- BRICK RED
BOOT TOPPING:- BLACK

NOTE

FLIGHT DECK MARKINGS AND DETAILS OF STARBOARD SIDE ARE SHOWN IN PHOTOGRAPHS

TWIN 4.5" GUN TURRETS
CRANE
STERN
4 - 3 PDR SALUTING GUNS
AIRCRAFT LANDING AID
AIRCRAFT LANDING AID
RADIO MAST (HORIZONTAL WHEN FLYING)
ANEMOMETER
WATER LINE
SHADING SHOWS FLIGHT DECK OVERHANG
"SEACAT" DIRECTORS—6
"SEACAT" LAUNCHERS—6
LIFERAFTS (WHITE)
LIFT
LIFT

FEET 0 100 200

H.M.S. Eagle

H.M.S. Eagle

H.M.S. Eagle

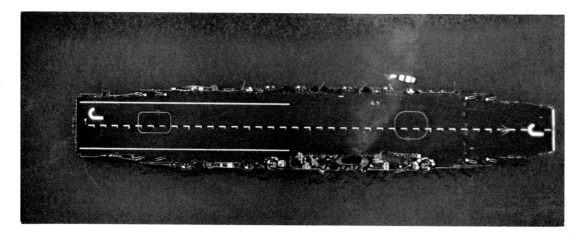

Wessex helicopters for the anti-submarine role. It will be seen, from the wide diversity of aircraft types, that the ship is really a self-contained small air force that is capable of going anywhere at short notice. To operate similar aircraft from the land requires a sophisticated base covering a large surface area which has to be secure. The *Eagle* and the other carriers offer all these facilities compared with land bases and, especially, with those bases whose security of tenure is doubtful.

LEADING PARTICULARS

Displacement: 44,100 tons (standard).

Length: 811 ft. Beam: 171 ft. (maximum width).

Machinery: Geared Turbines, 152,000 S.H.P. Speed: 31·5 knots.

Armament: Eight–4·5 in. D.P.; six–'Seacat' S.A.M. Launchers.

Aircraft: 34 plus 10 helicopters.

Complement: 2,750.

Ark Royal

1955

LAID down on the 3rd May, 1943, this ship was to have been called *Irresistible*—the name *Ark Royal* had been allocated to a projected larger carrier. However, when this larger ship had been cancelled, it was decided to perpetuate the famous name in this carrier under construction. With the war coming to an end and the advent of the jet aircraft, construction was slowed down; seven years after she had been

laid down she was launched on the 3rd May, 1950, and completion followed slowly on the 25th February, 1955.

She differed from her sister ship *Eagle* in that she had a side lift, the first to be incorporated in a British carrier, and a 5½ degree angled deck. Also new were the first steam catapults to be used by the Royal Navy and associated equipment—arrester gear and a more effective deck landing

H.M.S. Ark Royal

H.M.S. Ark Royal

aid. Her armament consisted of 16-4·5-in. dual purpose guns and quite an extensive array of 40 40 mm. guns.

During 1956 the forward port guns were removed to allow for a clearer flight deck. In 1959 most of the other guns were taken away along with the side lift so that flying operations would be completely unimpeded. Before her service is complete she will, in common with most warships, have other improvements incorporated. Gun armament is not at a premium in these type of ships, at the present time, as it is reckoned that there will always be other escorting warships accompanying an aircraft carrier.

Like our remaining other carriers, the *Ark* *Royal* has served, and continues to serve, overseas, and in particular around the potential trouble spots East of Suez; with her complement of fighters and bombers she presents, like her famous predecessor, a formidable deterrent.

LEADING PARTICULARS

Displacement: 43,340 tons.
Length: $810\frac{3}{4}$ ft. Beam: $112\frac{1}{4}$ ft. Maximum width: $164\frac{1}{2}$ ft.
Machinery: Geared Turbines, 152,000 S.H.P. Speed: 31·5 knots.
Armament: 4–4·5 in. D.P.; 14–40 mm.
Aircraft: 40 plus 8 helicopters.
Complement: 2,345.

Hermes   1959

THIS ship can claim the dubious distinction of having spent longer under construction than any other aircraft carrier. Laid down on the 21st June, 1944, she was launched on the 16th February, 1953, and finally completed on the 18th November, 1959. Originally she was laid down as a member of the *Centaur* class and would have been named *Elephant*. However, during the course of construction, various improvements and modifications were introduced to justify her being a separate ship from her earlier sisters.

Five post-war developments were incorporated into her design, and these were: the angled deck, steam catapults, mirror landing aid, 948 'searchlight' radar and the deck edge lift. The angled deck is $6\frac{1}{2}$ degrees to the centre line, as opposed to $8\frac{1}{2}$ degrees in the *Eagle* and *Victorious*, which is the biggest angle that can be practically contrived in a ship of this size. Particular attention was paid to her accommodation, which is air conditioned throughout.

Another important feature is that the latest system of remote control for her engines has been fitted. This, coupled with automatic feed for the boilers, enables the ship to be controlled from the 'citadel'. The 'citadel' is a self-contained section of the ship that is proof against radio–active fall-out; the *Hermes* can be safely steamed through an atomic cloud.

H.M.S. Hermes

H.M.S. Hermes

Although a long time was taken with her construction this can be vindicated, to a great extent, by her many modern features. During 1964 to 1966 a long refit was carried out to bring her right up to date. At the present time her aircraft types include the Sea Vixen (Night All Weather Fighter) and Buccaneer (Strike Aircraft. However, due to her smaller flight deck, it is not likely that the *Hermes* will be able to operate the much heavier and faster jets which may come into service. But, short of this, she is a very efficient ship—and certainly our newest carrier—and should serve right up till the time that the aircraft carrier is phased out. Even after this time she may well be useful as a Commando carrier, anti-submarine carrier or a maintenance ship.

LEADING PARTICULARS
Displacement: 23,000 tons.
Length: $744\frac{1}{4}$ ft. Beam: 90 ft. Extreme width: $144\frac{1}{2}$ ft.
Machinery: Geared Turbines, 78,000 S.H.P. Speed: 28 knots.
Armament: 10–40 mm.
Aircraft: 20 plus 8 helicopters.
Complement: 2,100.

H.M.S. Victorious

Victorious   1941

ALMOST thirty years old, this very much modernised carrier is the sole survivor of the *Illustrious* group and, as such, she is interesting, linking the past with the present. She was laid down in May 1937, launched in September 1939 and completed in May 1941, when she joined the Home Fleet at Scapa Flow.

Her first operational assignment would have been to escort a Middle East bound convoy on the initial stage of its voyage. However, this was cancelled quickly when it became known that the *Bismarck* was in the Atlantic. Sailing with the Home Fleet, the carrier was hardly prepared for the operation; she had on board a large number of dismantled R.A.F. Hurricanes and only 15 naval aircraft—six Fulmars and nine Swordfish. In the action that followed, these aircraft were employed on reconnaissance and in a torpedo attack on the 25th May, when one hit was obtained which resulted in the battleship having to close down one of her boiler rooms; the resultant lack in speed spelt the writing on the wall for her. Shortage of fuel prevented the carrier remaining until the destruction of the *Bismarck* on the 27th May.

During June the *Victorious* escorted a troop convoy on its initial stage of the voyage to the Middle East and, on the 4th, one of her aircraft sighted the German tanker *Gonzenheim*—one of the *Bismarck*'s supply ships—and as a result the cruiser *Neptune* was able to intercept this vessel, which scuttled herself. On the 13th, with Force H, she ferried 47 aircraft to Malta, of which 43 arrived safely; after this she returned home and was allocated to the Home Fleet.

Operations with the Home Fleet included the following for 1941. On the 30th July, 20 Albacores and eight Fulmars took part in an attack on Kirkeness, Norway. Unfortunately, surprise was lost when an enemy reconnaissance aircraft spotted the force; little damage was done and 11 Albacores and two Fulmars were lost. From

the 23rd August she took part in the escort of the first convoy to Russia; whilst in this Northern area her aircraft carried out two attacks against enemy shipping in Norwegian waters near Tromso and Bodo. On the 8th October, with Home Fleet ships in support, her Albacore aircraft carried out a successful attack on enemy shipping between Glom Fiord and the head of West Fiord.

Nineteen forty-two began with more Norwegian operations which included sweeps to look for enemy warships in very bad weather; due to this weather the enemy was not seen and three aircraft were lost. Continuing operations to provide cover for Russian bound convoys, her Albacore aircraft, on the 9th March, sighted the German battleship *Tirpitz* and attacked with torpedoes, but no hits were obtained. Between April and July the *Victorious* assisted to cover several more Russian convoys and then it was time for her to move on to another theatre of operations.

Leaving the Clyde on the 4th August with a convoy bound for Malta, the *Victorious* was part of the escort which included two other carriers, the *Eagle* and *Indomitable*. It entered the Mediterranean on the 10th and it was heavily assailed by U-boats, E-boats and aircraft; out of 14 merchant ships only five reached Malta and the *Eagle* was sunk. The *Victorious* was in fact hit by an aircraft bomb which, fortunately, failed to explode; this was the last convoy to be fought through before the island was relieved after the North African landings.

After taking part in these landings, during November 1942, an Albacore from the carrier, while she was returning to the U.K., depth charged and sank the German submarine U.517 off Cape Ortegal; 51 survivors were picked up by the destroyer *Opportune*. By this time the carrier was in urgent need of a refit after 18 months continuous war service so, on the 20th Decem-

95

H.M.S. Victorious

ber, she left the Clyde for Bermuda and the U.S.A. After a month's refit at the Norfolk Navy Yard, Virginia, she left there on the 2nd February, 1943, passed through the Panama Canal, and reached Pearl Harbour on the 11th March; her old Fulmars and Albacores had been replaced by Martlets and Tarpons.

Between March and August the *Victorious* was on loan to the U.S. Navy, which had lost four carriers in Pacific operations. Most of this time was in company with the U.S.S. *Saratoga*; British and U.S. squadrons learnt to operate together from the decks of both carriers. Together these two ships carried out many operations before the *Victorious* returned to U.K. in the September; at Liverpool she was taken in hand for repairs which lasted until the 4th March, 1944.

After a brief spell with the Home Fleet, during which she took part in an attack on the *Tirpitz* with other carriers, she joined the Eastern Fleet at Ceylon on the 7th July. She was soon back in action again on the 25th of that month when she took part in a sea and air strike on the Japanese base at Sabang, Sumatra; this was called Operation 'Crimson' and the Fleet went right up to Sabang and bombarded the harbour installations. The rest of the war was spent in the Pacific where she took part in many operations; on the 9th May, 1945, she was hit by two Japanese suicide aircraft and damaged but, within an hour, she was able to resume flying operations. It was necessary for her to return to Sydney for repairs which lasted a month; after this she was back at sea again and took part in more operations before the war ended.

Between December 1945 and January 1947, she was employed on trooping duties to and from the Far East and Australia. After a few months in the reserve she served from October 1947, to March 1950, with the Training Squadron and was then taken in hand for modernisation.

During this process, which lasted from 1950 until 1958, she was virtually rebuilt and her length was increased by 30 ft. and her beam by just over 7 ft. A fully angled flight deck was fitted, considerably increasing her width, as were steam catapults, new radar, new boilers and much other modern equipment including a different armament. Another long refit was carried out during 1962 to 1963; much of her service since then has been spent East of Suez, exerting pressure on trouble spots like Kuwait, Indonesia and Aden.

LEADING PARTICULARS

When first commissioned, her leading particulars were the same as the *Illustrious*. Note.

Displacement: 30,530 tons.

Length: 781 ft. Beam: 103 ft. (maximum width is 157 ft.).

Machinery: Geared Turbines, 110,000 S.H.P.

Speed: 31 knots.

Armament: Eight 3 in. A.A.

Aircraft: 25 plus 8 helicopters.

Complement: 2,400.

H.M.S. Victorious

H.M.S. Albion

Centaur Class

1947

OF the eight ships originally ordered in this class, the following were cancelled: *Arrogant*, *Monmouth* and *Polypheus*, together with the original *Hermes*—the present *Hermes* was to have been a member of this class but differs too much to be included. This class was designed as an improvement on the light fleet carriers which, basically, did not have sufficient speed for fleet operations. To remedy this fault, machinery was installed with nearly twice the power, giving an additional five knots in speed. In general appearance they are similar to the light fleet carriers, especially the bows, but are considerably larger in displacement and dimensions.

All three ships, *Albion*, *Bulwark* and *Centaur*, were ordered before the end of the war and were laid down on the 23rd March, 1944, 10th May, 1945, and the 30th May, 1944, respectively. The two earlier ships were launched in the spring of 1947 and the *Bulwark* the following year; the *Centaur* was completed first in September 1953 and the other two in May 1954.

Starting their lives as 'fixed wing' aircraft carriers, they had an armament of 32 × 40 mm. Bofors. However, with the advent of the angled flight deck soon after their construction, three twin 40 mm. mountings were removed from the port side. An interim angled deck was installed by the extension of the flight deck plating over the port side, where the 40 mm. had previously been installed.

During 1959 to 1960 the *Bulwark* underwent conversion to the role of Commando Carrier; the *Albion* was similarly converted in 1961 to 1962. Basically the *Bulwark* was not changed during her initial conversion, although the fixed wing capability—the aircraft arrester wires and catapults—was removed. Various alterations and modifications were made to render the ship suitable as an all-helicopter troop carrier; she

was fitted with, at that time, the most extensive air conditioning system in the fleet. In her initial conversion the *Albion* embodied a number of improvements and is able to carry a larger military force. Her extensive modifications included alteration to the angled flight deck and the removal of catapults and the arrester gear.

Both these ships carry 16 helicopters—at the present time these are Westland Wessex—and, at short notice and within their own resources, can adapt their aircraft to the anti-submarine role. The helicopters are large enough to lift most equipment including vehicles and artillery —the standard gun these days is the 105 mm. Gun/Howitzer which made its debut during the period of Indonesian Confrontation. Both the *Albion* and the *Bulwark* served in the Far East during this time; Marines and helicopters from these ships played their part ashore, manning lonely outposts in the Borneo jungles.

A considerable part of the original armament was removed to allow four L.C.A.s (Landing Craft Assault) to be carried aft. Both ships have sufficient stores and fuel to support the commandos in active operations ashore; with the helicopters and L.C.A.s the military unit can be speedily re-embarked when required. The Royal Marines, who are linked by long tradition with the Royal Navy, form the commando units in each ship which consists of about 900 men; in an emergency or on short haul operations this number can be increased considerably. Apart from the troops, the normal ship's company is just over 1,000.

The *Centaur* has not been converted to the Commando role at the present time. Her future, with more and more heavy jet aircraft entering service, may lay in the Commando role or the pure anti-submarine role with helicopters.

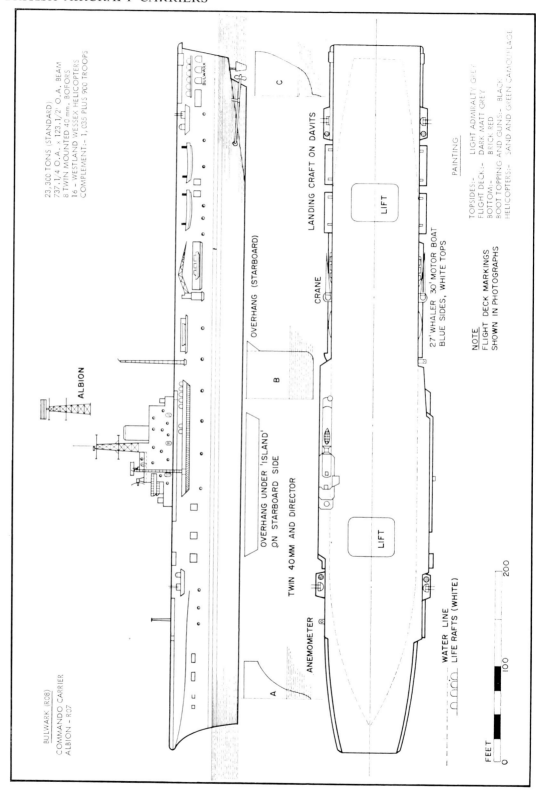

BULWARK (R08)
COMMANDO CARRIER
ALBION - R07

23,300 TONS (STANDARD)
737.1/4 O.A. × 123.1/2' O.A. BEAM
8 TWIN MOUNTED 40 mm. BOFORS
16 - WESTLAND WESSEX HELICOPTERS
COMPLEMENT:- 1,035 PLUS 900 TROOPS

ALBION

BULWARK

LANDING CRAFT ON DAVITS

C

OVERHANG (STARBOARD)

CRANE

LIFT

B

OVERHANG UNDER 'ISLAND'
ON STARBOARD SIDE

TWIN 40MM AND DIRECTOR

27' WHALER 30' MOTOR BOAT
BLUE SIDES, WHITE TOPS

NOTE
FLIGHT DECK MARKINGS
SHOWN IN PHOTOGRAPHS

PAINTING

TOPSIDES:-   LIGHT ADMIRALTY GREY
FLIGHT DECK:- DARK MATT GREY
BOTTOM:-   BRICK RED
BOOT TOPPING AND GUNS:- BLACK
HELICOPTERS:- SAND AND GREEN CAMOUFLAGE

ANEMOMETER

LIFT

WATER LINE
LIFE RAFTS (WHITE)

A

FEET
0   100   200

100

H.M.S. Bulwark

H.M.S. Albion

LEADING PARTICULARS
Displacement: 23,300 tons.
Length: 737 ft. Beam: 123 ft.
Machinery: Geared Turbines, 78,000 S.H.P.
  Speed: 30 knots.
Armament: Eight 40 mm.
Aircraft: 16 helicopters (greater capacity in
  Centaur).
Complement: 1,035, plus 900 troops.

H.M.S. Bulwark